RIPPLES FROM THE DARKNESS

THE COLLECTED
POEMS AND STORIES OF
GEORGE TYRRELL

"Ripples From the Darkness," by George Tyrrell. ISBN 978-1-62137-486-2 (Softcover) 978-1-62137-487-9 (eBook)

Published 2014 by Virtualbookworm.com Publishing Inc., P.O. Box 9949, College Station, TX 77842, US. ©2014, George Tyrrell. All rights reserved. No part of this publication may be reproduced, stored in a retrieval system, or transmitted in any form or by any means, electronic, mechanical, recording or otherwise, without the prior written permission of George Tyrrell.

Manufactured in the United States of America.

WITH LOVE TO ROSANNA AND FAMILY

RS

For

Mary Flad
With best wishes
from

George Tyrrell
(author)

Topical Selections

RIPPLES FROM THE DARKNESS: THE POEMS 1
PRELUDE.. 3

YOUTHFUL FOLLIES... 5

TALES FROM THE HOOD... 15

SHADES OF MADNESS 23

ROMANTIC INTERLUDES 35

WHEN LOVE IS GONE.. 43

DREAMS OF GODDESSES 49

WHERE THEN IS GOD?... 59

BEYOND GOD:... 79

SHUDDERS FROM THE SHADOWS: THE STORIES.. 95
PRELUDE.. 97

THE LITTLE BOOK OF HORRORS 99

INTIMATIONS OF THE HOLY 173

George Tyrrell
(845) 298-9507
doubters@lycos.com

RIPPLES FROM THE DARKNESS
THE POEMS

PRELUDE

Poetry lost broad popularity because of a gradual rift between poets and readers. Academic and professional poets continue writing to impress literary journals with few readers—the public be damned. For within erudite circles it seems a long growing fad became traditional, namely: make your poems as meaningless as possible; strive toward the clever word-play above all else, the more obscure and ambiguous the better. Small wonder most poets can never quit their day jobs. Who will buy writings no one understands?

On the other hand, normal readers seek words making sense, phrases with meaning, experiences they can relate to. With this fact in mind it is actually possible to write good poetry without using words that blind. Truths themselves, when lucidly written, can become aesthetic (even ambiguous) in their own right. Reality becomes mysterious enough no matter how clearly we seek to express its secrets. We will find this especially true in the spiritual and metaphysical poetry of the last sections as the poems reach their apex. Since true poetry does flow from a shadowy place, we should seek to unveil—not further obscure—life's secrets.

The following will be collection of poems and stories taking us on an odyssey through labyrinths of humor, love, madness, and beyond. Like ripples in a pond we will

3

find the literature expanding as it rolls outward—starting with simplicity and humor, moving outward toward climactic crescendos. So now let the ripples flow visibly from the darkness......

YOUTHFUL FOLLIES

A TRIVIAL TRIOLET

When the trivial becomes important,
the important becomes quite trivial.

Trifles become magnificent
when the trivial becomes significant.

Seeking excellence is different
from striving after drivel.

When the trivial becomes important,
the important becomes quite trivial.

WHEN THE MAGIC DIED

There came a time when
Santa and the Tooth Fairy
died…..
and I laid my toy soldiers
aside,

and could no longer believe
in the magic of angels –
and found even fairy tales
lied….

"Was God dead too?"
I'd ask the nuns in school.
And they'd send me from
the classroom to my seat
out in the hall.

So that's how *all*
the magic died.

CRAZY BONES

I was the kid they called
"Crazy Bones"…
gangly, scrawny, couldn't
walk without tripping…
Something had to change….

Down in the gym the boxers
taught me to skip rope,
do the Russian kick-dance,
pump iron, punch the bags…

Then came the day
I really felt free.
I could float like a
butterfly, sting like a bee…

From that day, woe
onto those
who made fun of me….

A BEER FOR GRANNY

Down in the basement
we'd drink, and sing songs,
play cards, and shoot dice
the whole night long.

But we'd sometimes get visits
from granny upstairs.
She'd come down at all hours,
catch us unawares…

Then she'd stare at us sternly.
"Are you boys drinking beer?"
And if we hid the bottles,
she'd find out just where.

Then she'd snatch my beer bottle,
hold me off with her crutch.
"I'm doing this for your good
'cause you're drinking too much."

She'd then chug down the beer
as quick as she could,
then chug down another—

all for my own good!

One night she came down
when we ran out of beer.
"Where's that beer, Sonny?
I know it's hid near."

"But we're out of beer, grandma.
There just aint no more."
She hit me with her crutch…
knocked me clean to the floor.

"Don't you ever hide beer
from me anymore!"

So from that one night on,
we were wise to her game.
'kept a spare beer handy
for when granny came.

KATY DID IT

At the Half Moon Saloon we all gathered with glee.
Killer Katy on furlough was a sore sight to see.
In that same saloon lounged the gang from uptown
eying us with contempt as they sloughed their drinks down.

Then the shouting died down; all were quite and still.
Katy showed how marines made a bare handed kill.
But in his excitement, he drank the wrong beer.
It belonged to a guy from the gang sitting near.

Then that huge guy loomed up, and all froze in fear.
and he leered down at Katy. "You just sucked up my beer!"
"Then, I'll buy you another. It's cheap; what the heck."
"No! I'll just rip off your head and drink from your neck."

"Now look, you behemoth, I didn't suck your beer!'
"You did, and what's more I think you're a queer!"
But Katy stood upright; showed no sign of fear.
"You're too drunk to know that your end is near."

Head to head, lip to lip, they both slobbered and growled,
till all gathered 'round in one bloodthirsty crowd.

It was swift; it was sudden. And that's all she wrote.
Katy broke the beer glass and cut the guy's throat!
Blood squirted all over. Police entered the bar.
Katy hid in the men's room. He didn't get very far.

When they grabbed him he said,
"I didn't do it! You're wrong!"
But when they dragged him outside to the katydid's song.
"Katydid! Katydid!" the katydids sang.

T'was my last reunion with Katy and the gang.

YOUTH

Youth,
in all your naïve
brutality....
seeing all things
distortedly through
your misleading mask
of innocence.

Youth, if stumbled
upon the wisdom
of the universe -
with a gibbering laugh
would cast it aside
for things
more glitteringly
trivial

TALES FROM THE HOOD

NIGHT WALKER

You can see them each night
on the seamy side of town
sauntering, prancing
past bar-rooms, dance halls,
after-hour diners.....

One of them strolled up
to my car window.
"Lookin' for a good time mister?
I can give you pleasures
your woman won't allow."

What lay behind those vacant eyes?
What secret horrors suppressed
within that drugged and dying soul?
Hell, even a whore was a virgin once.

So I said to her,
"Here's some money, sweetheart;
and one less John to desecrate
God's sacred child in you."

Then, with her mouth agape,
I left and drove off
alone...

CHRISTMAS EVE

Shimmering Christmas lights
reflect in empty streets
past the midnight hour.
Warm lights in windows
blink out into darkness
one by one.

Cigarettes glow
from dark doorways
as the hookers step out again
into the night, shivering,
pulling their short coats
tightly about them.

The roar of a car….
Staccato shots echo
through stony streets.
Sounds of footsteps running…
Another ghetto youth
lay dying in a gutter…
Harlots hurry away
toward brighter lighted
sidewalks.

Later, with the light of dawn,
church bells ring, sounding
their unwitting death knell
to another urchin lost
in empty streets…..

The vampiras
and seductive witches
of the dark
promenade
back to their hovels,
their death dance
and man-watch
awaiting the next lethal
orgy of the night.....

LONELY WALKING BLUES

I wake every morning
feeling real low down.
And I feel even worse
when nighttime comes
around…

When I first met you woman,
you had that red dress on.
You could do the sexy shimmy
and shake it all night long.

I gave you plenty money
each and every day.
Then you found another stud
and went your merry way.

Now I'm broke and beat this
morning
walking down the street.
Got to hustle up enough
to get a pint of sneaky pete.

I got the blues….
Got those lonely walking blues…
Because I'm beat without you baby.
Now I got nothing more to lose.

FAT MOMMA BLUES

She's a big fat momma,
she's got hair like a horse's main.
First time I met that momma,
she was stepping off
that dark night train

Yeah, she's big and fat,
she's got dancing feet
She can jump to the rhythm
of a boogie beat.

And when she puts that red dress on,
she keeps the men and bulls
a charging all night long.

She shakes it like jelly,
'cause jam never shook
like that.
I love that momma
'cause she's so big and fat.

Yeah, my big fat momma
is awful good to me.
She knows how to take me
out of my misery.

SHADES OF MADNESS

PRELUDE TO MADNESS

Freud was wrong.
Defenses are not neurotic.
Pure madness ascends
when our defenses exist
no more.....

Where then would be
the solace of our myths?
Can mortal minds truly
withstand
the end of all absolutes,
of all cherished dreams
dissolving
into an ever-widening
black hole of the psyche?

From those unholy depths
the monster called
Nihilism
can then rear
its frightful faces of
futility, meaninglessness,
despair....

From there, the absence
of all purpose,
rendering all we value
senseless,
all we believe in false,
all high hopes disparaged.

At that time we know
we are cast adrift
but briefly,
only to perish
in a cosmos that cares not
and knows us not.

There then exists naught
but the frightful choice
of creating our own meaning –
or else making that blind leap
of faith into society's
ready-made beliefs

of the absurd....

BLOOD RED WINE

I dreamt of drinking
blood red wine
beneath a scarlet sky…
My mind
in fading violet glow
sunk down
where thought-forms lie…

A weird world pierced
the glowing gloom…
Red clouds turned
blue black night…
Through pearly fields
a silver road
wound through
the white moonlight…

Strange whispers beckoned:
"Walk this road
and leave all cares behind…"
As in a trance, I tread
the shimmering byways
of my mind…

Then, an angel blocked my way,
refused to let me by…..
My eyes flew wide and startled
to the blazing blue of sky…

Then I saw God's face once more…
His voice was at my side.
The glowing Presence
saved my soul…..

the night I would have
died….

A WITCH'S SONNET

The death scene was sad.
She lay crumpled and old…
They said she was mad,
or so it was told.

They called her a witch.
She made brew and cast spells.
'made dolls from black pitch;
'raised the devil from hell.

No one now to console.
no one now feels forlorn
for this poor old lost soul
who died here all alone….

I laid a red rose upon her lone grave
and prayed up to God her poor soul be saved.

NECROMANIA

Strange apparitions in a
graveyard....
Shimmering shadows in the
moonlight.

Misty, whispering forms hovered
over gravestones
decomposing in gruesome stages
of decay
like the corpses rotting beneath. .

Then there were the wailings....

And it seemed I heard
the murmurings of
loathsome rites echoing forth
from some dark magician....

It was then I saw
a shuddering shroud
fluttering from a tomb's
open door,
partially hiding its murky depths,

Then the necromancers came...
entering the tomb
with lighted torches.

And the wailings came louder,
and the wolves howled
back at the wind....
the macabre song of night.

Later, the moon
took on the red of dawn.
Scarlet shadows crept
through purple gravestones;
the bloodshot eye of sun
peered into the mist.

The necromancers
filed out from the tomb in
grim procession.
What ever it was,
their gruesome deed
was done.....

CROWS

A barren tree on winter's night.
Naked branches swaying
as dark silhouettes
in frigid moonlight.

A black, shuddering shroud
descends.

The branches are again in bloom,
now with a thousand fluttering wings.
The crows have gathered to converse,
their "caws" echoing shrill in the night.

Later, in red of dawn
the sky blackens with crows ascending
The tree again stands barren,
now baring only....
the secrets of the crows.

ROAD KILL

A crow stood staring at me,
bloody intestine swaying
from its beak.
There seemed a glint of evil in its eye.
If it could speak,
it might tell me things I could not
bare to know.

ROMANTIC INTERLUDES

ORIENTAL DREAMS
IN HAIKU

Behind silken veils
your face seems oriental,
stark white in beauty,

Darkness descending…
Torches born in processions
illume our chambers.

Shadows of color,
as a great jeweled moth alights
onto the jade shrine.

This night in a dream
I behold your sleeping face
shinning in the stars.

The dark sky glows blue
before the dawn arises
Stars sparkle the waters.

Now the dawn arrives…
Buds bathed in golden glow
unfold their splendor.

A shining dewdrop falls,
awakening a butterfly…
It opens its wings.

You open your eyes…
Your fair arms unfolding
for our sweet embrace.

SOUL'S ECHO

In vain I searched
the endless sky.
Now who can show me
thoughts on high?

         I

Where comes this sound
that seems so near,
a voice I cannot see
but hear?

          ...Here

An echo voice
sounds in the night!
From what source comes
such strange delight

          ...Light

In this bleak chamber
light is dim.
Could this light
come from within?

          ...Within

Yes, deep within
I sense you solely.
But tell me, just what are you
wholly?

          ...Holy

Are you the deep
and holy light
that oft inspires
what I write?

                    …Right

Then I have questions,
gentle glow.
Are there things
you do not know?

                    …No

Then tell me what
swooped from above
and smote me with
a silken glove?

                    …Love

Through you I pray
my doubts be ended.
Is my quest for true love
ended?

                    …Ended

Of other loves
that you could show one,
could it be
I'll never know one?

                    …No one

But love brings pain,
how well I know it.
Should I then keep it
or forego it?

                    …Go it

When fears and doubts
start to forsake her'
how can my love
then overtake her?

        …Take her

A purer heart
I'll never find.
But how can I know
she will be kind?

        …Be kind

If she and I
be not love's toy,
what moments will we
most enjoy?

        …Joy

You've had, I pray
sound truths to tell.
Now that I know,
I'll guard her well.

        …Guard her well.

        Yes,

        Guard her well….

NIGHTTIME THOUGHTS

Late at night
when my work is done
and I lay my books aside,
my thoughts begin to wander
through dark trees
and hills outside.

They fly across the city lights,
and a sleeping forest too,
and float up a familiar road
to rest at last with you.....

While you lay asleep
in your darkened room
and think that I'm away,
my thoughts creep
in there with you
to watch you where you lay...

And in my thoughts
I am there too,
so before they take
their flight,
I tiptoe to your bed
sweetheart
and there kiss you
goodnight.

But late thoughts soon
grow weary,
my eyelids close, and then
such thoughts turn
to pleasant dreams,
and there we meet again.

If I ever had to travel
to places far away,
my thoughts would cross
an ocean
and with you they would stay.

And if I had to leave this life
there'd be no need to cry.
For if you thought
and dreamed of me,
I'd always be alive….

In a hundred years
we'll both be gone
from this world of love
and pain,
but somewhere
in another realm
we'll meet and love again….

For in the land of thoughts
and dreams
true lovers never die….
They live on and on forever
In castles in the sky…

Late thoughts oft turn
to fancy, dear,
but this I know is true:
My fancies are of just one love
and that, my love, is you….

WHEN LOVE IS GONE

THE MUSIC FADES

Suddenly....
all music fades to
dissonant tinkling;
all beauty ebbs
in murky shadows,

with true love now
a laugh,
and God
but just a lie.

Now poetic words
become as scarlet
wounds;
my pen slices shreds
of all I loved...

The sun shines warm
in the summer sky...
But why have I grown
so cold...?

NIGHT RAIN

Night rain in the city….
Across the mists
of neon streets,
cold wind gusts
in watery waves.

My reflection in the street….
A man in a raincoat
flowing down manholes
into underground waters.

Past loves gone by….
Left to surge down drains
into darkness,
or collect in quiet puddles
waiting for the sun.

Tears and raindrops
bead my glasses….
Seeing fragments
of a lost love falling
from the cold night sky
and trickling
into empty streets.

IMPOSSIBLE DREAMS

A delicate princess
atop a glass mountain
beckons in woe
to yon knights below…
Noble champions
on bannered stallions
snorting fire,
ascend with spiked hoofs
far up the glassy wall
only to finally slide
and clamor down
again into
the brash bowels

of normalcy…

STORMS OF LIFE

Storms of life roll in like waves
unfurling fiery scrolls.
But each will pass.
Then comes the calm,
the period of repose.

So when those storms of life surge in,
no need to be forlorn.
Ride out each wave with inner calm.
Then surge ahead with inner storm.

DREAMS OF GODDESSES

ODE TO DIANA

Your forms are ageless
and forever changing....

Now you are Rea,
with high throne
at your back
and panthers
at your side
The dark depths
of the forest
ring with the cries
of your worshipers.

You are my queen.
Now with the cruel eyes
of a tiger,
a beauty
turned barbaric.
Forgive me if I fail
to hear the words
you speak.
for I am struck dumb
and helpless
by your beauty.....

LILITH

She howls with the wind....
Seducer of sleeping men.
Devourer of children.
Ancestor of Eve.
Rejecter of Adam.
Provoker of God....
Behold the very first woman,
the great she-devil—Lilith.

Equal to Adam in every way.
no subordinate would she be.
Was cast from Eden for defiance
to God.
Banished to the desert regions,
the wild forests, the dark waters.
Now running with the wolves.
Now the tempest of the stormy sea.

Lilith remains the fierce rage
brewing in the breast of
Woman
since the time of the Goddess:
when women ruled
in the Golden Age
before men's wars,
and the desecration of our great
Earth Mother....
Lillith will one day return
to bring our fierce race to justice.

Already proclaimed
in the Holy Book of Revelation:
"When a Great omen appeared
in the heavens—
a woman clothed with the sun
and crowned with stars
was with child.
And she cried out in her pangs
of birth"—
in her throes of birthing
the hordes of demons to be
unleashed upon this Earth
when arrives those final days.....

EVE

My belly swells
with the moon.
Cursed by God
since time began....
Heed this omen:
I am Eve
— your Mother.

When first I raised
my shaking hand
toward the forbidden
fruit of knowledge,
all the heavens trembled
in ominous anticipation.

And a jealous God
cried down to me
that He was the only one
to know the great mysteries,
that He would exile us
from Eden's
ignorant bliss
into the world of reality....
and death....

But I ate from that fruit
of truth
and the real world
was born.
From no man's rib
came I....
Beyond Adam
and all creation,
I emerged not
as an afterthought....

I am the culmination!

MOTHER GOD

O Celestial Womb
eternally outpouring:
Thou heavenly Mother God,
propagating
new creation
throughout all the heavens....

You were the mother star
giving birth to our system.
You are also our great mother
Earth,
your patriarch the mighty sun.

As our blue orb, Earth,
your womb is alive
with internal fire.
The rocks are your bones,
the waters your blood,
the soil your skin,
the flora your hair,
the air your breath,
all creatures your children of life.

Your human reflection
is every loving mother with babe.
A spark from your womb's inferno
gave life to every unborn soul.

And we are your children of consciousness
free to honor and enhance your holiness,
or to desecrate your grace to
become exiled from your beauty
forevermore.....

END OF A DREAM

I dreamt of finding a secret place,
a place to be never found again.
A sacred garden
with shimmering pool
fed by a stream winding
through willowy trees
and wild flowers.

By the pool was the shrine,
of a golden goddess.
The sunbeams danced.
An ember of light sparked her eye.
She began to stir.
I was bedazzled by such beauty.

But then the sky grew dark.
A cloud's shadow descended
upon the garden
bringing shivering, brittle,
ice-clear night.
It was when reality
vomited from the earth.

And I awoke —
to a gray, wet morning…
Raindrops turn to teardrops
as they bead upon my window.
And I lie here staring….
thinking about gardens…..

WHERE THEN IS GOD?

WHERE IS GOD?

From that misty time
when our brows retracted,
when our brains became intact,
never again
would human nature change.
With progressive tools of genius,
but the morals still of beasts,
we continue to deceive
and remain deceived
in utter darkness.

"Where is God?" Nietzsche cried,
"Are we all his murderers?
How can this be?"
When was God exiled
to now exist outside nature
and ourselves –
and yet remain created
in our own apelike image?

Yea, if no God exists,
then only we are gods –
but dying gods,
with no immortal souls….

Or will we someday know
something within our souls,
not hominid like ourselves,
but a shining beacon
to our true Source
in life's infinite Mystery?

THE INVISIBLE SPECK WE BE

Why shout "God & Country!"
when the Bible's God sees nations
as fine dust?

Why believe ourselves the apex,
with our entire solar system
an invisible speck
at the fringe of a galaxy
with billions of suns,
the galaxy itself invisible
in a cosmos with billions of galaxies?

Yea, what an invisible speck
we be!
How count for anything at all?

Yet Scripture says:
"even hairs on each head
are all counted".
And science confirms
such intricate care
from DNA down to quantum
infinitesima.

Even when human born,
each life starts one-celled,
then swims in the womb
with gills of fish,
then come hair and tails
like our mammalian cousins.
Hence, part of all life are we.

And originally stardust formed,
no strangers to the stars are we.
So we're parcel of something
far Greater than we.
In the words of the poet, Pope:

We're part of one stupendous
whole whose body is nature
and God the soul.

PERSONIFICATIONS

O Lord, forgive my idolatries
due to my human limitations.
You are everywhere,
but I worship you here.
You are without form.
But I worship in these forms.
You need no praise,
yet I offer you these prayers
and salutations.
O Great Mystery,
forgive these idolatries
due to my human limitations...
_____ Prayer of a Hindu priest

Most cannot like an Einstein
grasp the majesty of the cosmos,
or like a Buddha
tap the profoundest source
of the psyche.
So it seems Divinity mercifully
assumes images of sacral
personhood within our fantasies
to compensate such limitations.

How can divine personifications
become catalysts
to spark rebirth in persons,
so even the child
can find salvation in tune
with the greater cosmic scheme?

Verily, the cosmic womb
of the heavens
finally gave birth to Earth
as our own Great Mother
whose image evolved
from pregnant stone figurine
to divine mother and babe
and the male/female counterparts

Iana & Dummuzi,
Ishtar & Tammuz,
Cyble & Attis,
Isis & Sarapis
Madonna and Child –

All bringing nature's
constant resurrection
down to hope for our own
resurrection as well….

And distilled from
the great Mystery of creation
was worship of sun and storms,
of phallus and bull,
of high god,
finally the one Father-God
procreating great faiths three.

And just as stone-age hunters
partook from the flesh and blood
of the cave bear
to receive its powers,
and Greeks partook from the wheat
and wine of Bauchs
to receive the ecstasy,
so too did Christians
eat the flesh and drink the blood
of their own God to be saved.

All became blessed and cursed
for these human limitations....

THE FACE OF GOD
DESCENDING

It was said:
to gaze upon God's face
brings instant death.....
And so it was
in the beginning....
when Earth was born

of cosmic turbulence:
from flaming debris
of exploding starburst,
a molten ball of fire,
lightening streaking
through poisonous gases,
meteors falling
sulfuric liquids steaming,
all preceding any hint of life.

Herein blazed a face of God
no mortal could behold
without annihilation.....

But the face became
finally benign,
would impartially
rain and shine
upon good and bad alike.

Then at last the birth of humanity,
creatures who might still contain
a spark from the inferno
of God' creation.
Hence, Theophilus'

"Logos Spermatikos",
the seed of the Logos
in humankind....

But a seed grown far
from its fruition....

EXILED FROM EDEN

The ego brings on
separateness,
mortality...
our cosmic Source
forgotten....
We each then cherish
our apartness and dread
its loss
with its final surrender
required.

Whenever I perceive a purer
part of nature,
I feel a subtle sadness
at my apartness from it,
a longing to cross the void
between myself and
the nature outside myself.

Even the splendor
of trees, grass and sky
seem but a baroque veil
separating me from
a profounder essence.

When in dim antiquity
were we first cast out
from our animal innocence?
When did our cerebral fruit
of knowledge
first take dominance from
the primitive brain?
The cost was banishment
and exile...

Forced to steal fire from the gods,
we, like Prometheus, must suffer
the vultures of painful self- awareness
consuming our entrails.
Like Adam, we must endure the knowledge
of non-being.

Part animal, yet unable to return
to instinctual bliss—
part angel, yet unable to attain
immortality--
we, each of us, remain trapped
between the jungle of the beasts
and the heaven of the gods....

forbidden to enter either gate.

THE DARK SIDE OF HA'ADAM

"Curse is the very ground because of you."
The fear of you shall be upon every living
beast of the earth, every bird in the air,
upon everything that creeps, and all the fish
in the seas." (Gen. 3: 7, 9:2)

And so it has been
since the birth of
Adam:
parasite of the planet,
pillager of earth,
poisoner of waters,
polluter of air,
mass murderer
of all species,
including his own.

Socrates' rational
creature —
yet Nietzsche's insane
creature —
the product of reason
severed from Earth's
greater wisdom,
the deeper ecology
from which all life
was formed.

Yea, the true face
of evil is that of
lewdness,
power-lust,
violence,
deceit.
And it is always
a human face.
For Satan is in truth

the Dark Side of Man.....

BE BLIND TO
ARMEGGEDON

Some call Satan
this world's ruler.
I say it's Mammon,
his great enticer,
and Ideology,
his great recruiter.

Hence the birthing
of history's macabre
generations of antichrists
and their religions
of the damned—
better named—

Greed,
Powerlust,
Homicidal Holiness,
all in the name of a
god, who is the father
of all lies indeed.

So must we walk by
faith,
not by sight,
lest the true nature
of the world and God
drive us
truly mad?

IN SATAN'S NAME

The name of Satan,
drawn from the darkness
of our *own* souls,
becomes the goat
bearing our *own* horrific sins –
the projection of *human* evils
too unspeakable to own.

Nay, the dark side needs
no disembodied spirit;
nor did the devil
make us do it.
We ourselves do it all…
and always on our own……

WHERE THEN IS HELL?

The cosmos has its
shadow side
bordering on the edge
of chaos and nothingness.
Yet, can chaos,
or cosmic darkness,
or the nothingness of
non-being contain
a realm called Hell?

Or are chaos and darkness
instead
the pregnant pangs
of unborn potential,
the turbulent wombs
of new being
and more becoming?

Nay, the realm called Hell
can lurk only where there be
consciousness.
For without awareness
there can be no suffering,
without suffering no Hell.

"The mind is its own place.,"
said Milton's dark angel,
which can make
a heaven of hell and a
hell of heaven indeed

I say: Change you mind.
Make your thoughts kind.
Walk by faith and not by sight.
Then you'll escape Hell,
whether wrong or right.

My faith
is called
Seeking
after Truth. My place of worship the Temple of all life...
My high priests, rabbis, and gurus – life's experience: and
the wisdom, discoveries, and revelations of wise and holy
ones of all faiths and all times. My own private chapel will
be where I
can dwell
in solitude
to meditate,
until I hear
the holy
whisperings
of my own
sacred soul.

BEYOND GOD

WHO AM I?

With eternity existing
before my birth,
and eternity forever
beyond my death,
how strange
to exist at all....
or at this very time.
Who am I really?
I seem like a fleck of foam
upon some stormy sea...
a fleeting moat of awareness...
a brief spark
from an eternal flame...
a wayward light lost
within endless shadows
of eternity...
a universe
within a universe...
a seeker of life,
of love,
of truth...

Dust...

THE DEATH OF ULTIMATE CONCERN

Each secular school stops mute
at the threshold of non-being…..
I say stop not at that
forbidden gate;
for therein the truth
lurks hiding…

Or should we instead
while away
our brief time here
dignifying the mundane,
the trivial,
glorifying all things
perishable?

If so, then cursed be
the perpetual pragmatist
trapped
in an endless drudge
of expediency.

Damned the
Pollyannaish humanist
not knowing his dark side
seeks oblivion.

Doomed the existentialist
whose self-absorption
blinds him to the splendor
of the cosmos.

Blighted the cynical positivist
ignoring all of love,
transcendence,
and the mystical. ...

Reduced to ruin
the postmodernist
losing all noble visions
of beauty, goodness, truth.
For with nothing to believe,
he is ruined indeed.....

Without ultimate concerns,
would death
render each brief life absurd?
Would even immortality,
without purpose,
become a morbid tedium
begging for death's mercy?

Therein lies the crux
of the human predicament:
repressing the growing
anguish of non being
by pursuing life's trivia.
And finally facing the
crushing despair

of never having lived at all

BEYOND
WHAT WE CAN CONCEIVE

How brief our egos,
these separate selves....
Could there exist a state
beyond such transience,
beneath and beyond
all conceivable dimensions,
a state transcending our
awareness
as ours now transcends
that of a microbe?

Such God's-eye perspective
might see each finite ego as
but a snagged flea struggling
mightily in a cosmic web
to save its little life;
for it can conceive of no higher
existence.

But the mystics see liberation
akin to a spark returning
to its flame...
a raindrop returning
home to the sea....
a crumbled courtyard wall
now letting the sun shine
everywhere without shadow....

The Egyptian Book of the Dead
speaks of self-liberation as
becoming a sibling of the moon,
a child of the stars,
revolving in the heavens,
rising with the sun....

Maybe death is merely
a stepping out of time
into an Eternity
beyond what we can ever
conceive....

HOW CONSCIOUS ARE WE?

The intelligence man seeks amidst the
apelike recesses of his brain lies beyond
the reaches of dictionary language
_____ Alfred North Whitehead

Conscious awareness is a strange state of being.
Where will it go when our brains leave this scene?
Will it go out like a light or remain in the air
like some energy field dispersed everywhere?

Did it sleep in the rocks before life was formed?
Or dream in the flowers before beasts were born?
It did stir in the creatures before human beings?
Was it fully alive when we entered the scene?

How conscious are we? Are we fully aware
of all the strange mysteries lurking out there?
Can we smell what a dog smells or hear all he hears?
Like a bat in its cave, can we see with our ears?

Like the humble crayfish, can we sense the moon's tides?
Can we see like an insect through multiple eyes?
Are there colors before us, or just waves of light?
Where do they go when day turns to night?

Is the mind is still just dreaming, not yet quite awake.
To truly be conscious, how much would it take?
Perhaps we are part of a far greater Mind.
For lack of true knowledge, let's call it Divine.

Nay, the last word in knowledge can never stop here.
For this bubble in space/time could soon disappear,
to merge back with the cosmos from which it once came –
to again know its Source and end this brief game.

MIND & MATTER

The opposite of a profound truth
can be another profound truth.
_____Neils Bohr

Complimentarity
sought equality
for opposites in reality.
Mass can turn to energy,
then back to its carnality.

So need the mind be tied
to flesh's tyranny?
Could it ever cut loose
and then fly about free?

Our neurons are matter
with a field-frequency.
But the field becomes conscious,
and a mind is set free.

Is mind's depths abysmal?
Can it trace its strange course
back to the Mystery,
its own cosmic Source –

far back beyond the birth
of the sun
to the time mind and matter
existed as one?

There's miracle in matter
starting back from afar when
our minds first evolved
from the dust of a star.

THE MIRACLE OF BEING

The idea of being....
existence itself....
confronts the very origin
of nature's miracles,
and asks the ageless question:
Why should anything exist?

If some spark-accident
ignited quantum
infinitesima,
why not just fizzle back to
nothingness
and be no more?

But the lonely Void,
before creation,
brewed alive with potential
both lawful and creative:
potentials of endless complexity,
potentials of all life
and consciousness –
even beyond what we know now.

How name this mysterious Void
in the beginning?
The Causeless Cause?
Ground of all Being?
Tao that cannot be named?
Clear light of the Dharmakaya?
Shimmering Void of Shunyata?

Meister Eckhart bade our return
to this Source
through: "Discovering the Spirit
from which the heavens are driven,
and by which everything
grows and flourishes…..
Then enter into the Vortex –
the Source where the Spirit
originates –
and lose all sense of number
and becoming."

THE MIRACLE OF BECOMING

From the miracle of being
emerged the spectacle of
becoming....
If the first infinitesima
faded not to oblivion
as it should,
why then eternally evolve
into ever-increasing
complexity?

Like the Phenox –
born from turbulence,
constantly dying
and resurrecting from chaos,
each time more spectacular
than before –
existence kept endlessly
progressing
until life and we ourselves
finally evolved
from the very dust of
a dying star....

Hence, the revelation
of the mystic Van Ruysbroeck:
"From the rest and stillness
of the Godhead,
emerged an outpouring
manifest in differentiation."

Or the proclamation
of Theophilus:
"From the Logos Endiathetos
of the cosmic womb
was born the Logo Prophosikos
of all creation
proceeding forth in all its glory..."

EINSTEIN'S
MYSTICAL VISION

What is material?
does matter
really matter
in the grand
scheme?
Or is it nothing
but atomic-electric
enigma
inter-changing as
ephemeral energy
immersed as a warp
of impurity
in an extra-
dimensional
continuum?
If all this be true,
then nothing else
could be true except
the spiritual,
and the mystical,
Then we could all in part
ourselves be spiritual beings.

COSMOS OR CHAOS?

Some claim cosmos just chance amidst chaos.
Some say strict laws rule our brief lives.
So are we but as leaves just blown in the wind?
Or are we instead but blind robotoids?

Acts of atoms and persons seem random and free.
But from God's stern eye view, just how free are we?
Are we trapped in a whole that determines its parts
and where everything stops and where it all starts?

Is there a great scheme that directs this foul play?
Are we but its actors with nothing to say?
Is the cause in the future? Are we its effects
who cannot do a thing to save our poor necks?

Could quantum physics solve this for us?
Let complimentatrity quell all this fuss.
We may be both drops in this vast, stormy sea
and waves of potentials rolling eternally.

We may each play a part in directing the whole,
while the whole plays its part in saving each soul.
So let us not wonder if we're bound or free;
It will all pan out ...

.....in eternity....

SHUDDERS FROM THE SHADOWS
THE STORIES

PRELUDE

In *The Little Book of Horrors* the ripples conversely roll from the light back into darkness. Again they start small—but ever expand until they reach their crescendos in the shadows of the supernatural. Here we will eavesdrop on a study of evil, from the humorous to the horrific, as we voyage through the dark side. Perhaps it's time to lighten up a bit. But once escaping the absurdities of *Dr Frogenstein* and the diabolical *Doorway* we will encounter the serious side of the Satanic.

In "A Tale from the Crypt" we might scorn or pity the necrophile Orlaf. In "The Night Has Thousand Eyes" we may find how alien beings from a dying planet could inhabit an Earth alien to their own bodies. "The Return of Elisabeth Bathory" asks if diabolical potions and demonic possession could be possible this very day. Our final "Journey through the Dark Side" reveals how the system that creates war can make monsters of men.

With *Intimations of the Holy* the ripples emerge again into the light, reaching their crescendo with the coming of the Christ in our time. With "A Rose in Spanish Harlem" we will come across a surprising parable of chivalry over intolerance in the hood. And in this world of uncertainty, we might find refreshing intimations of truth from "The Seeker". Finally "The Second Coming" asks the question: If Jesus ever did return, would the powers that be crucify him again?

97

THE LITTLE BOOK OF HORRORS

FROGENSTEIN'S MONSTER

Dr. Eric Frogle, noted chemist and zoologist, came upon an opportunity he could not refuse: the prospect of capturing the rare specimen Phyllobates Terribillis, a frog whose skin excretions can be used as cardiac stimulants and anesthetics in surgery. Proper precautions would be necessary however, for the frog's skin also contains a slime capable of causing hallucinations and psychosis. Its poison was in fact used in the blowguns of the dreaded Chocó natives.

The expedition started in the mists of early morning. In the jungle, slithering things wriggled past cautious feet, crawled on tree trunks, hung from branches. Soon the thicket became obtuse; the carriers had to hack their way through with machetes. Faces from ancient statues peered through gnarled vines, ruins reclaimed by the jungle, relics of a strange civilization once conquered by the Incas.

The arduous search was already starting to seem futile. But as the third week ended, the expedition became suddenly blessed with a stroke of serendipity. For there standing upside-down on a tree trunk was a tiny, brightly colored frog staring with beady eyes. For all to behold, lurked the dreaded Terribillis crouching there for the taking. The frog's deadly toxicity bade all to approach with care.

Dr. Frogle netted it with one swift swipe and dropped it into a ready container. If there was one in the area there should be more; so they continued their searching, and after a day or two did manage to net enough of the species to produce significant quantities of the desired chemicals.

But as the expedition headed back to the compound, Dr. Frogle began feeling strange. He remembered one tiny frog brushing against his bare arm as he captured it. He washed the slime off as soon as he could, hoping he'd be lucky and not affected by its hallucinogenic poisons. But then why was he feeling so peculiar?

The tangled brush began taking on a shimmering aura and started undulating around him. Frogle commanded the procession to stop while he sat against a tree to rest. The jungles musty smell became intense. Its screeching, roaring and bellowing became deafening. Then the visions came......

A ghostly Inca shaman sprang from the bushes dancing menacingly about; he then put his curse on Frogle with a serpentine pointing-stick. Then Frogle amazingly experienced himself on all fours stuck onto a tree trunk staring downward. Then he was swiped into a net by something looking like a giant frog. He was suddenly trapped in this huge container and giant froglike creatures were peering down at him with big beady eyes.

He was then carried off to a laboratory where he became a specimen for experimentation. He was about to be dissected. "But I am not a frog!" he cried out. "My name is Doctor Eric Frogle! I work for Toxicological Pharmaceuticals! You cannot do this to me! Please believe me! I am not a frog!"

But Frogle was tied down onto the table and dissection began. The laboratory came alive flashing, sparking, and buzzing. With electric terminals on the sides of his neck he was being slowly transformed into a huge froglike monster. And a mad frog scientist cried out: "It's alive! It's alive! God help us, it's alive!"

It was then he awoke shuddering and screaming. Those in the procession were all staring at him strangely. He suddenly ran toward them all, striking the containers from off the pack animals shouting, "Set the frogs free! Set all the frogs free! For I now know how they feel, you see…. because I was once a frog! Do you understand? I was a frog! I now know just how they feel! I know just how they feel!"

To this very day there exists a strange scientist. Late at night on a foggy hill you can see the lights flickering and flashing in his laboratory. They claim he is bringing dead frogs back to life -- perhaps even creating new life with organs of the dead. Some say he's attempting to transform a frog into something ghastly human. One passerby even heard him exclaim, "It's alive! It's alive! God help us, it's alive!"

So goes the story of a mad scientist, now known to the villagers around that diabolical hill as—Dr. Frogenstein.

THE PUSILLANIMOUS DOORWAY

As I sit here trying to compose my memoirs, an ominous figure keeps blotting out my mind. It's eclipsing any recollection of my sane, normal life. Always that infernal Door that diabolical Gateway to the very depths of Hell! But I must compose myself!

We discovered it quite by accident, you know, while arranging flowers in the greenhouse. It was a rather large greenhouse with many sections to breed different species of orchid. Did you know the African Orchid has in it a design actually resembling a bee's vigina so to attract more bees to its pollen? Oh, but I'm getting off the subject now. It appears whenever I try to think of the Door, my mind disintegrates and goes elsewhere.

But if I'm to keep what little sanity I have left, I must put it all back into perspective... A large greenhouse has a kind of inner sanctum, you know, a middle section where the prize specimens are kept. It was in that very inner chamber we one day came upon a peculiar looking door we hadn't noticed before. No! No! I can't go on... I mustn't speak of such things anymore! But then again I must! I must! You think me insane going on like this? Maybe I am; for it seems some strange, evil thing is compelling me to tell you the rest.

It was a strange looking door. I thought it was glass but it seemed to ripple and undulate if I looked at it long. At the time I thought it was just the sweat making my eyes bleary, for I had been working quite hard.

Well, something from somewhere silently warned me to not open that door. My wife, Ethel, who was working by my side, noticed my reluctance and tried to open it herself. But her hand seemed to disappear through it as though it were made of something just thicker than air.

"It looks like something you can walk thorough", said she. And before I could stop her, Ethel stepped right into and through the damned thing pulling me in with her!

Well, it was the strangest thing you ever did see. It looked like a weird world of vapor and light. And in the middle of the swirling mist stood a giant orchid, one of tremendous size. There it stood, pulsing and glowing in that horrible haze. "What a magnificent specimen!" said Ethel. She walked toward it as though entranced.

I grabbed her and cried out, "No, Ethel! Don't go near that thing!" But she was a big woman and pushed me aside so she could see it better.

"My God!" said she, walking right up to it. "It's so beautiful! I can't really believe my eyes!" Then she began actually stroking the huge flower.

No Ethel! Don't touch it!" I shouted. But my warnings were in vain. Suddenly this flowery behemoth stretched out its petals to embrace Ethel.

"Isn't it darling", said she. "It's actually hugging me."

And hug her it did. Its tendrils wrapped all around Ethel lifting her high in the air. Then it was pulling her inward toward something like a vaginal shaped mouth. And with one inward thrust Ethel screamed and was no more! She was enveloped into the monster's entrails like some giant insect, as it were!

Oh God! I headed for that facsimile of a door and dove through it landing again in the greenhouse. When I looked back, the door seemed to have disappeared; but I dared not approach it too closely lest I too be sucked into that diabolical domain of Hell!

The worst part of the whole thing now is: Nobody believes my story to this very day. Many times I took the police to that evil entranceway. But no one could find it anymore. I believe they are merely afraid to find it. They certainly would be afraid to enter into it if they did find it. That's why I now call it the Pusillanimous Doorway!

As I now sit here in this rubber room with those in white periodically watching me, I know they are all afraid – afraid of what they might find if ever they entered that ominous Gateway to Hell... But I know it's true. And when I get out, I'll be there to find you Ethel! For I'm no longer afraid. No, I 'm no longer afraid Ethel! No! Ha Ha Ha Ha Ha! No longer afraid!

A TALE FROM THE CRYPT

Orlarf, the sweeper, lumbered through his chores at the mortuary oblivious to the thundering storm outside. For him this was a happy place, a place where everyone -- be they billionaire or bum –were finally equal, all of them finally inferior to him at last. No not one of them, not even the women could look down their noses at his deformities anymore.

He stopped sweeping a moment to stare into a mirror and reflexively cursed his humped back, his shriveled leg, his deformed face. He spat at the mirror and moved on. But then no one cares about that here, he thought. He giggled to himself and hummed tunelessly as he went about his work.

Yes the women, he thought..... It was their rejection that always hurt him most even as a child. He thought of the ways they would ignore him or show their repugnance, some subtly with some quaint taunt or remark. But that was when he was young and still thought someone might accept him as a natural man.

But here it's the women who are repulsive now. Here even the beautiful ones have finally lost their haughtiness and pride as they lay mute, mindless, senseless, unable to resist the advances of even the rats and maggots... all doomed to rot into something far more disgusting than he.

Why if he became amorous with them now, he would be doing them a favor.

As he worked his way to the room of the crypt a tingle of gleeful anticipation crept through him. For tonight's new entry was a beautiful raven haired girl. She was tall, statuesque in life, finely bred, the kind he always craved most... but who would be most repulsed and rejecting of him were she alive. But now.... He giggled foolishly and lumbered into the room of the crypt.

Here lay the bodies to be embalmed. They lay on separate tables each covered with a white sheet. Yes, he could have his way with any of the women here, and they never protested when he did. He shuffled toward a white shrouded slab in the far corner of the room. With trembling hands he grasped the sheet and slowly, fervently pulled it back off the still form beneath.

He stood for a time staring agape at the delicate, white figure lying naked before him. "Why, she's like a fragile Venus sculpted in ivory!" Guttural utterances sounded deep in his throat; a string of saliva hung motionless from his slack lips... With trembling hands he hesitantly reached out and touched her body, at first cautiously in one spot, then all over with feverish abandon.

Finally he stepped back and with little, lusty squeals began removing his tattered clothing. Then naked, heedless of his deformities, he lumbered toward the corpse and with surprising agility leapt upon the slab where she lay. The lights of the mortuary blinked off, then on again as lightning flashed and thunder boomed outside.

A sudden chill of fear gripped the hunchback but for only a moment. "The very gods are angry at old Orlarf tonight, my lady," he cackled. "For they never intended someone like you for the likes of me." He threw back his shaggy head and laughed shaking his fist and wagging his finger mockingly at the storm's rumbling and flashing outside the window.

Then, shaking with a desire intensified to delicious perversion, he kissed the lifeless, unresisting lips again and again.

At first he thought he was imagining it in his excitement... But then his back hairs rose in frightful awareness. Each time he'd breathed into the lifeless mouth, he'd felt the cold bosom rise.

Slowly, he pushed himself up with arms trembling so badly he for a horrible moment thought he couldn't separate himself from the corpse. Finally he forced himself to look down and saw the bosom slowly rising and falling. He stared for a long time, hypnotized, unable to move....

Then a cry of panic stifled in his throat as he saw its eyelids flutter, then slowly begin opening to finally reveal the veined whites of pupilless eyes. An eerie cry uttered from her bloodless lips, at first low, then highly pitched into an ear- piercing scream...

Somehow overcoming his paralyses, Orlarf half slid, half fell to the marble floor. There he crouched on his haunches watching petrified....

Her hand jerked once. Her leg slowly, shakily slid from the slab, touching her foot to the floor. Then her body very slowly, disjointedly began to rise....

Whining sounds emitted from the hunchback's throat as he tried to get his fear-stiffened muscles to move him away.

She began rising unsteadily to her feet. Her pupils, now no longer rolled back, stared crazily about the room, her face taking on a hideous expression. Then she finally fixed her insane stare upon the crouching man. She extended her arms toward him uttering a long, mournful cry and started approaching him slowly.... outstretched arms jerking spastically as she approached him.

The lights went out again. After a maddening moment of pitch blackness a series of lightning flashes lighted the room revealing the naked female—now tall, stark white, raven haired, eyes black sunken holes.... She seemed to dance crazily before him in flickering, stroboscopic madness.... Her shaking, silvery hand was about to touch him....

The room was in blackness once again....

He tried to cry out, but his voice came only in a shaky rasp. "Keep away! Damn you! Don't you touch me, you cursed vampiress from Hell!" He arose on trembling legs in the blackness and slid along the wall in the direction of the door. But then he stumbled into something that blocked his way. He reached down to feel a metal table and something cold and pulpy beneath a sheet.

The lightning flashes revealed the shroud actually rising in spastic jerks before him, then it was slowly sliding down off a gnarled hag sitting upright and convulsing rhythmically, guttural moans belching from putrid lips.... He could smell her fetid breath on his face...

With a shriek of terror, he lurched wildly through the blackness toward the door; but his legs tangled in his mop and pail and he flew crashing into another shrouded table, and fell whimpering to his knees....

The room lighted up once more as a woman's blue-white arm fell out from the shroud; its jagged fingernails sliced down through the man's twitching face leaving chalky, bloody streaks before it came to rest on his throat.... The room was black once more....

Screeching and shrieking the man—now gone mad—scrambled on all fours in the direction lf the door.

Finally, his trembling hand found the door, then the doorknob. He turned the knob and pulled. The door remained shut. He turned the knob and pulled again, and kept pulling. The door wouldn't budge. He pulled even harder—and the knob came off in his hand.

With a wail that echoed throughout the mortuary, he collapsed against the unmoving door and crumbled babbling to the floor. "Mother of God, please help me!" were the last coherent words he said as the strobing lightning again revealed the tall dead woman gliding slowly toward him still emitting eerie cries as she gestured frantically with outstretched arms....

And with each flickering flash, a more ghastly horror revealed itself. Now the shrouded table was coming toward him, wheels creaking, the blue-veined arm hanging out , swinging stiffly, its curved, claw-like hand pointing at him... moving ever closer....

Now the lightning lit up the next table revealing the old hag again sitting up in spasmodic jerks, guttural moans belching convulsively from rotting lips; her table also began rolling toward the naked hulk of terror cringing and babbling on the floor....

All the horrors approaching him danced eerily each time the lightning flickered crazily about the room.

Now he was sure all the lifeless women he was good enough to service... actually doing them the favors...were coming for their revenge. God! Even the dead were repulsed by him now. No! This could not be... He threw back his head sending a howl of utter despair reverberating throughout the crypt....

Then all was silent at last, except for the distant thunder as the rain stopped falling, and the first pale rays of daylight entered the windows of the morgue.

———

Later that day the mortician was having dinner with a new partner in a nearby restaurant. He breathed a sad sigh of relief. The crypt was finally straightened out, and the ambulance and police had left at last. He shook his head gravely.

"Too bad about poor old Orlarf. He was a bit feeble minded but he always did a good job cleaning up the place. It'll be hard to replace him after that incredible incident."

His partner looked a bit perplexed. "The poor man actually died from fright, you say?"

The mortician grimaced. "Yes, it was quite dreadful. We found him squatting naked in his own filth, hair turned completely white, his face a mask of horror..."

"He was naked you say? Don't you think that a bit odd?"

The mortician looked bothered. "The whole thing's very odd. No telling what a man might do in the grip of panic and horror."

"What about the girl? Do you think she'll ever be sane again?"

It's hard to say," said the mortician. "She was suffering from acute shock when we found her. Finding oneself awakening under a shroud in a crypt with corpses laid all around you is an unspeakable experience." He paled slightly. "No one had any idea she was cataleptic. She had carried nothing to identify it on her. Nor did she have any discernable pulse or heartbeat at all when pronounced dead. Even rigormortis begins to set in such cases, you know. Extraordinary!"

The colleague shook his head. "It's a wonder she pulled out of it at all. Why, you could have embalmed her! My God!"

"Yes, a horrible thought. She's quite lucky in that sense. Sometimes it takes something like mouth to mouth resuscitation or the like to revive such cases. But who could have done that without knowing?" The mortician looked bemused.

"Her rising up from her shroud and roaming about in her shocked, incoherent condition must have been what frightened Orlarf literally to death," mused the colleague. "His heart must have been not very sound, poor man."

The mortician shook his head slowly. "There appears to be other factors, which might finish off any superstitious person, even if he had a heart of iron."

"Other factors?"

"Yes, for instance the position of at least one corpse showed some rare necrokenetic phenomenon must have taken place in the night."

"Necro... kinetic? You mean to say a corpse actually moved?"

The mortician nodded grimly. "We found the corpse of an old lady frozen into a sitting position. The lightning rod's grounding wire must have blown through the open window. It was tangled around her metal table; and when lightning struck…"

"You mean to say, the charge from lightning could actually make the corpse move?" The colleague looked incredulous.

The mortician nodded. "That was indicated by burn marks on the corpse. There have been similar rare phenomena such as gas escaping from a corpse actually creating a sound."

The new colleague was aghast. "How extraordinary! Almost unbelievable!"

"Yes, but quite possible. The entire scene - tables and bodies in disarray, sheets partially off, arms hanging down, and such – all indicate poor Orlarf must have been skittering about in panic. This would be understandable if he witnessed the woman rising from her slab and wandering about, and the corpse sitting upright, along with the lights blowing out, and the opposite door-latch locking him in.…"

The colleague winced. "It's no wonder the poor, feeble minded man was frightened to death!"

"Yes, quite a gruesome series of coincidences."

"Coincidences?" The colleague again looked incredulous. "All those macabre events occurring last night... just mere coincidence? It makes you wonder..."

The mortician looked at his colleague queerly. "Of course it was coincidence, man. What could that poor, wretched man ever do to deserve such a fate? Why, I don't believe he would ever have done harm to a living.... soul...."

THE NIGHT HAS A THOUSAND EYES

Unable to sleep, she sat gazing into the flickering night sky. The night was sultry and the garden breeze felt cool as it fluttered through her hair and billowed her negligee. Just as she felt drowsy enough to return to bed, something strange caught her eye. It looked like a star much brighter than all the rest and it seemed to be getting bigger and brighter all the time…

It was actually moving, and coming in her direction at fantastic speed. She remained transfixed, unable to take her eyes from the ever growing, gleam in the sky. As it came ever closer it appeared something like a glowing orb surrounded by radiant auras. In a sudden fit of panic the woman tore her eyes away from it and forced herself to rise and run into the house on trembling legs

The man awoke with a start as she pulled him frantically from the bed. "What in hell's wrong with you, Janet?" he stammered as she led him stumbling to the porch. "Look out there. For God's sake, Eric, look out there!" she said gesturing wildly at the black, starlit sky.

He peered blearily up into the glittering cosmos. "What the hell are you talking about Janet? There's nothing peculiar out there now at all." She forced herself to look upward toward the spot where it was. It was no longer there. She scanned the heavens frantically, but the thing was nowhere to be seen.

"But it was out there, Eric, I'm telling you it was out there!"

He took hold of her and shook her gently. "Janet, get hold of yourself. Just calmly tell me what you saw."

"It... it was like a light, a glowing ball... moving at tremendous speed... then suddenly it just stopped and began coming toward me. It kept getting closer... bigger... brighter... It kept glowing and pulsing. I got the awful feeling it was coming for me, Eric. Oh Eric, that thing was after me!"

He held the sobbing woman firmly. "Listen Janet; the sky is full of falling stars on a summer's night. It might have been a meteor or one of those fire-ball phenomena. It could have been anything. There's no point of overreacting to such a thing as that."

She finally felt calmer as he slipped his arm around her and led her back to the bedroom. Eric was an astrophysicist for goodness sake. So he should know far better than she what was up there. She smiled up at him weakly. "I really can't understand why that thing frightened me so.... why I have this awful, eerie feeling. I guess I'm acting terribly stupid."

They got under the covers and she snuggled close to her husband who soon began dozing. She lay there awhile thinking about what she saw and how foolish she must have seemed for overreacting that way. Finally, feeling secure in his arms, she began to doze...

In less than a minute she opened her eyes again trembling in fright. Mustering all the courage she could, she cautiously closed her eyes again—but opened them wide at once, cold terror spreading across all her features. After the third try, she bolted upright in panic.

"Eric!'

"What now?' he moaned from the depths of sleep.

"It's... it's still here! It's still here with me!'' she wailed sobbing uncontrollably as she clutched onto him in desperation.

He rolled over, regarding her again through bleary eyes. "Janet, you know I've got to be in the lab early this morning. So tell me just what in hell is wrong now?"

She spoke slowly, hesitantly in a forcibly controlled voice. "I'm still seeing it! I see it glowing and pulsing every time I close my eyes. Each time I can hear its awful humming. Each time it keeps coming closer and closer... keeps getting brighter and brighter. Every time I close my eyes it comes ever nearer. Something terrible is going to happen if it comes any nearer. I feel it... I just know it Erick!" She began sobbing again.

He held her tightly looking bemusedly at the shaking, fear-wracked woman he always knew to be so composed, the one whose calm demeanor he always regarded a stabilizing factor in his life.

"It must just be some kind of after-image phenomenon, some eidetic optical illusion," he said to calm her. "You must be under some kind of stress. It's already daylight. I'll take half the day off and we'll contact Dr. Higgins when he opens in a couple hours."

———————

The doctor gave Janet a complete physical exam and tested her eyes thoroughly. Then he talked to her for a long time. Afterward, he took Eric aside. "This case is quite extraordinary, Eric. Janet's physical health is sound and her eyes seem in excellent condition. I've never observed or learned of such a lasting eidetic afterimage. Then when we take into consideration the strange humming and the image appearing progressively closer each time..."

"Then what in hell could it be, Doc?"

"Frankly, as I already suggested to your wife, the only answer left seems to be hallucination -- closed eye eidetic and auditory hallucination similar to the kind elicited by some psychotropic drugs."

"Nonsense, My wife does not take drugs, and she's surely not crazy!"

"If neither is the cause, there might be a way to curtail her attacks without further treatment necessary. All she may need is a good night's sleep and the knowledge she can do so without experiencing the hallucination. Therefore, unbeknown to her I could prescribe a strong sedative that would put her quickly to sleep without the experience."

"I... I'm afraid that sounds like our only immediate hope doctor. But what if it doesn't work?"

"Of course if the attacks persist after that, there's no option left but psychiatric help."

Eric got the prescription for her on their way home. He told her it would make the image go away. Once he got her home and gave her the medication he made her promise she would take it and rest through the afternoon until he returned from the lab. Then kissing her goodbye he left to catch up on some overdue work.

The scientists were called to a meeting. It concerned a slew of UFO sightings, and strange behavior among some of the people involved in the sightings. Eric was especially interested, since his wife was acting like one of those people. Then came the startling news that satellite telescopes received signals of serious disruptions on a nearby stellar planet. Moreover, the more advanced roving telescope spotted mysterious objects that seemed to be leaving that planet and heading in unspecified directions.

They discussed the seeming impossibility of traversing interstellar distances, even at near light speed without taking centuries. But then there were theoretical ways of utilizing time warps, worm holes, and extra dimensions that far surpassed our current knowledge of technology. But what of intelligent beings perhaps thousands of years advanced beyond us? Look how fast our technology improved even within the past 50 years... The past decade...

At the close of the meeting, the minutes read accordingly:

* Any reports of disk shaped objects will probably be bogus, since the *original* term "saucer" described not the vehicle's shape but its skipping motion through our atmosphere. The crafts originally sighted more resembled a V shape similar to our own stealth vehicles.

* Just as our stealth aircraft are invisible to radar, vehicles advanced enough for interstellar travel could also be invisible to all other electromagnetic spectra as well, including visible light – hence, completely invisible, unless they wished to be seen.

* Motives of such advanced intelligence could be largely beyond our ken.

* However, since our Earth is a rare, life giving planet among the horrid conditions of planets known so far, it could certainly attract attention from intelligent life forms, especially if their planet became no longer habitable.

* Modes of taking over Earth by such intelligence could well be beyond our conception, and might not be even noticed until too late.

* To settle here they would have to in some ingenious way adapt their bodies to be compatible

with an atmosphere g force, and pressures different from those on their own planet.
* If such highly developed intelligence could communicate with humans at all, it might be telepathic
* Bringing their communication down to our level could be analogous to our communicating with a low grade ape, a rodent perhaps.

After Eric had left for work, Janet promptly flushed her medication down the toilet. She'd be damned if she was going to take anything to make her close her eyes again. But then how long could she hold out like this? Cigarettes and coffee were not working anymore. After a long while, and despite heroic efforts, her eyelids finally shut involuntarily as she drifted off into twilight sleep....

The huge pulsing orb was there again. This time it finally stopped, looming large in front of her. A dark, murky hole became slowly lager in its center until a form drifted out of it through a vaporous, lime laden atmosphere. With a sound of crackling energy, it began moving toward the petrified woman. In mortal terror, Janet tried one last time to throw open her eyelids.... but she could not.

The form came ever closer... enveloping her now. She let out a soundless scream echoing through recesses where night terrors dwell. Mercifully her horror-stricken awareness began to fade, then disappear. The psyche that was once Janet was now dissolving into an infinite expanse of everywhere, and nowhere... and finally was no more.

In its place emerged an alien consciousness far too expansive, far too mysterious, complex, and profound for any human being to know.

When Eric rushed into the house early that evening, he found Janet sitting by the patio's glass doors gazing into the darkening summer sky.

"Hi baby, did you finally get some decent rest?"

She turned to him and smiled. "Everything now is fine. No more need to worry …"

Eric felt relieved, but then strangely uneasy. "Your voice," he said. "I can hardly understand you." There was something about that smile… and those eyes… He must be under some kind of stress himself, he thought. He actually imagined he was staring into the eyes of something inhuman. How stupid! Abruptly, he arose and fixed himself a drink.

"Have you heard, Janet, the apparition you experienced is thought to be widespread among other people as well?"

"Yes," she murmured, but her "mouth" remained closed. "It is occurring over the entire world… And it will happen again tonight, and every night, till there will be no more left…only those of us, my dear…"

"What? My God, I can hardly hear or understand you. What happened to your voice, Janet?" It seemed not like speech, but … something… telepathic?

"I said nothing you might understand, Eric." She arose and moved toward him.

Damn, he thought. Her feet seem to be hardly touching the floor. What the hell's wrong with me anyway? He gulped down his drink.

She reached for his hand. Her touch felt icy; slight electric impulses went up his arm.

"Why don't you and I sit out by the garden tonight, Eric? It is so nice out there on a summer's night. Then we can just relax and gaze out into the starry night sky…."

THE RETURN OF ELIZABETH BATHORY

From the small window of a padded room red eyes stared through wild webs of hair; blood drooled from her lips. "Release me from this tower! Do you not know who I am? I will have you all flogged and flayed alive! How dare you have the gall to desecrate me this way?" Her screams resounded throughout the halls of the asylum.

But let us start from the beginning. Eva Nadasdy was a plain, timid woman in her thirties. When not working long hours as a nurse, she spent time reading to escape the monotony of her life. One night she came upon an interesting biography. It told of a sadistic, 17th century noblewoman who tortured hundreds of female servants to death in the Balkans. She was the Countess Elizabeth Bathory. The Countess actually tasted the women's flesh and bathed in their blood. It was said the blood baths kept her skin smooth, white, and translucent ---so lovely in fact, she never seemed to age.

What made the biography especially interesting to Eva was the Countess' husband's last name. It was Nadasdy, the same as her own. Even more intriguing, Eva herself was of Romanian descent. Could it be possible she was related to the royalty back in those medieval days? The thought was exciting. She wondered why her parents and grandparents never spoke of this woman. Her parents did come to America from that same area of Hungry.

Then she thought of the Countess' retaining her beauty and never aging. It couldn't have been just from blood. She must have had a hidden secret. Eva then looked into the mirror. Her hair looked dry and lifeless, her complexion sallow, pocked with acne. God, why did she look so haggard? No wonder men never gave her a second glance. That was the reason she stayed an old maid all these years. Yes, it would be such a great miracle to look like a beautiful woman. What price could she herself be willing to pay?

When she called and brought up the subject of the Countess Bathory to her family, her mother said: "There are things our family must never speak of, things that have a curse on them. Your grandparents believe strongly in omens and so do we. Some things are better left unsaid."

But this cryptic answer sparked Eva's curiosity even more. She was sure there was more to herself than being just some nondescript drudge. She was due for a vacation, so why not visit her great grandmother in Hungary? She was a wise old woman who lived in the Bathory area, and could certainly show Eva the connection of her roots there.

Preparing for her visit, she wired her great grandmother at once. Greater excitement: The old woman's reply indicated she was not as closed-lipped about her ancestors as was the rest of the family…..

———————

Eva started the vacation on a plane to Hungary to visit her grandparents. When she arrived they were glad to see her and treated her royally; but they remained closed mouthed about the old-time Bathorys and Nadasdys. Eva noticed the concealed looks of horror and shame on their faces. They finally told Eva her great grandmother had become ill and gave her the address of the hospital they had just returned from visiting.

Eva told her grandparents she would return, then hired a cab and rushed to the hospital herself and found the room where her great-grandmother lay. The old woman was glad to see her great granddaughter at last. Eva was fairly adept in the Slovak language and the old woman could speak some broken English. So after answering many eager questions about her parents in the states, Eva finally got around to asking about the nature of her roots in the old country.

The old woman was too weak to speak at length, but told Eva she was indeed a descendent of the Bathory and Nadasdy line, that Eva herself was in fact really a Bathroy who as a baby was adopted by the Nadasdys! This revelation made Eva suddenly dizzy with shock and unbelief. She actually had in her the blood of Elisabeth Bathory, something she would never get over from that time on.

The old woman then revealed someone who could tell her the whole story of the Bathorys and Nadasdys. Her name was Blanca Horivitch, a folk healer who was said a descendent of Bathory's evil witch, Dorka. She then gave Eva Blanca's address in Bratislava saying, "She and I were friends. I would often buy her potions. Tell her you're the great granddaughter of Ava Nadsdy, and she will welcome you."

Eva prayed the old lady be blessed, then left with apprehension in her heart, and found herself taking a bus-ride to Bratislava. From there she took a cab to the rural outskirts where Blanca lived. The old woman was the last of a long line of rural medicine women and herbal healers. Her potions often worked wonders. She also gave tarot readings and drew up astrological charts for locals and tourists in the area. It was said she could also cast spells...

———————

Blanca regarded Eva with piercing eyes. Her hand began trembling on her twisted cane. "Are you sure you want to hear things better left unsaid... unspeakable things that brought horror and shame to your family for all those generations?"

"But what is past remains past," said Eva. "How could any of it harm us or be blamed on us after all the centuries gone by."

The old woman's piercing stare took on another direction, as if gazing through mists of time. "There are gothic legends whose forbidden truths lurk beyond all fable with their horrors...." The fire from the potbellied stove cast sinister shadows on the old woman's face as she spoke in a shaking voice filled with omen and foreboding....

"It is true. The Nadasdys take their name from the male descendents of Elizabeth and her husband Ferenc Nadasdy. But the Countess was strong willed enough to also keep her maiden name, Bathory as well. The descendents of that name now go by the name, Bathor, to avoid the stigma. "

Eva felt enthralled. "So, then I am really a descendents of royalty! I actually have noble blood in my veins!" The old woman's body was now shaking in resonance with her voice. "Royalty, yes; but the bloodline is far from noble. There was madness in that line from earlier royal inbreeding. Though brilliant and adept in three languages, Elizabeth was said to have the falling sickness, and was overcome with spells and murderous rages."

Eva found herself gasping. "So all the legends are really true?"

"She was often possessed by demons, and even worshiped a cat demon from Hell," said Blanca, her eyes became fixed as she stood gazing deeply into a forbidden past... "Yes, at times she would dress as a man with her evil lover, Anna Darvulia, a female incarnation of Satan. At other times she was overcome with ravenous urges for torture and murder... Do you know of the hundreds of poor women she tortured and slayed?"

"Is... is it true she bathed in their blood and never aged?"

"She indulged in evils even too horrid to be logged in the archives of her trial. Yes, after tasting the flesh and blood of her victims, she would a actually bathe in their blood and rub it into her naked skin, and that skin took on the soft whiteness and translucence of a new born babe...."

Eva was swept with a feeling of both horror and intrigue. "But how could just blood perform such a magical spell on one's skin. If blood really had such power it would be known by now."

The old woman shook her head. "It was not the blood alone. Along with the old witch, Dorka she concocted an elixir, a creamy potion from their witches brew. When mixed and rubbed on the skin with the blood, it was said to magically remove all wrinkles, all blemishes while the skin tightened and softened to a baby's delicate sheen. And that's the way Elizabeth always appeared."

Eva now felt keen interest. "Then why not use just the ointment? Why the blood as well?"

Blanca again shook her head sadly. "The ointment did not work fully without the blood, nor did the blood work alone. Both were needed together to create the black magic of eternal youth."

"But how do you know all this, if it was not recorded in the archives?"

The old woman's face seemed to darken with the wisdom of ages. "We folk witches have knowledge of spells, potions, and foul acts committed in darkness... knowledge passed down from generation to generation throughout the ages of time. Nothing within the shadows of evil in this land escapes our awareness for long."

Eva found herself becoming more strangely obsessed with the mysterious ointment that created beauty and long life. "Then do you know what became of the elixir... where it is now?"

The old woman shuffled away shaking her head and waving her finger ominously as if warding off evil spells as she spoke. "You do not want to know its whereabouts. The ointment carries an omen of evil. All who coveted it came to ill ends or went mad. It comes with a curse, which craves the blood of the innocent."

"But it's not a living thing; therefore how can it commit evil on its own? Evil can be committed only by persons, can it not?"

"Nay," said the old one, "The elixir carries the evil within itself."

"Then do you know its history?" Eva found herself desperately craving hints of where this potion, this creator of lasting beauty, had gone, where it might be even now.

The old woman seemed to apprehend Eva's motives. "I will tell you only its history of damnation, so you will understand the danger and why you must forget it and cease any craving for that which would ultimately destroy you."

Eva became hungry for any hint of the elixir. "Please tell me about it what you will."

Blanca studied the younger woman awhile as if again assessing her motives, then began to tell her tale. The lights flickered in the cottage and an ominous rumble of thunder shook the ground. The old woman paused, head cocked, eyes shifting wildly as if sensing an omen. Then she continued…

"Back in those days of old, Elisabeth's cousin, Thurso, the powerful Prince of Transylvania, raided Bathory's Castle in Cachtice. It was a black and stormy night. The Countess and her wicked attendants were caught in the act of torturing naked servant girls in the tower. Blood and dead bodies were strewn about. The evil doers were rounded up and taken away to be tried for their heinous, damnable acts.

"But the deformed servant and torturer Janos Ujvary managed to hide and avoid capture at that time. Needing money for his escape from the land, he took the formula of the evil ointment with him and finally sold it to the folk witch Helga on the outskirts of Transylvania and went on his way.

"But Janos was later caught just the same, and tried with the rest. All the wicked servants were finally tortured and burned alive. Elizabeth Bathory was sealed for life in her own torture chamber in the tower of Cachtice Castle. She started rapidly aging, and died there four years later.

"Meanwhile, the witch, Helga, who was growing old, began experimenting with the ointment on herself. She mixed it with the blood of sheep and pigs. It worked for awhile; she began to lose her wrinkles and look younger than before. Seeing its effects, peasant women came to Helga to buy the ointment along with her other potions and charms.

"But there was soon an epidemic of madness and peculiar behavior among the peasant women of Transylvania. Some murdered their husbands. Others killed their own babies, even drank their blood. The witch Helga finally went mad and took her own life.

"The ointment then fell into the hands of Helga's oldest daughter, Olga, who carried on her mother's witchcraft. She also started looking younger and younger, but also began acting evermore peculiar until she too finally went mad, and began using it the way it was originally intended by the Countess Bathory.

"Soon there was again a rash of missing peasant girls in the valley. Many were found in hidden places dead with their bodies drained of blood....

Finally the suspicion of both peasants and authorities fell upon Olga herself. It was said the soul and ghost of Elizabeth Bathory possessed this peasant witch whose beauty was becoming legend....

"With the villagers and authorities in pursuit, Olga took flight to Bathory's Castle in Cachtice, and hid in the underground passages. Some say she hid among the bones of Bathory's victims still buried there. Olga was finally found hiding in the crypt. She was tried, then burned alive.

'It was said other peasant witches flocked like vultures around Olga's cottage to find the coveted formula before the authorities burned it to the ground. Then came the plague of 1679, followed by the great flood four years later. In the chaos that followed, the events concerning the evil ointment and the murders were forgotten."

Eva listened to it all with intense interest. "And where did the formula end up, Blanca. Does anyone now know of its whereabouts today?"

The old woman looked grim. "It should have been burned and destroyed a long time ago. It was removed from Olga's cottage by a witch shrewder than the rest."

Eva's apprehension began to overwhelm her. "Then pray tell, where does it now lay hidden at this time?"

Old Blanca eyed Eva suspiciously, penetrating the younger woman's thoughts. "You too now seem entranced by elixir's power from just hearing of it. It had

132

that effect on many people, hence its long wake of destruction. Nay, young lady, that is one secret I must take with me to my grave."

Eva felt disappointed; but she knew she must snap out of the spell this story put on her. After all, the good witch was right. No good could come of playing with such accursed magic as that. But then, how much of it was superstition and old wives' tales, and how much was truth?

Blanca appeared to have one of her dizzy spells. "I'm afraid I'm getting too old," she said. "I believe it's time for my nap." Eva helped the old woman into the bedroom then hugged her before helping her into bed.

"Thank you, Blanca. Now I'll let you rest while I call a cab and be on my way." The old woman nodded and went off to sleep.

Lost in thought, Eva tripped on something, then braced herself on the wall near the fireplace. To her surprise a small, hidden door opened from the wall. "I must have hit a secret trigger." Peering inside, she saw an old book. Feeling her back hairs rise, she brushed the dust and cobwebs from the book and opened it. The pages were yellowed and brittle but the Slovakian writings were readable.

As she carefully looked through the book's pages, it seemed a kind of diary along with recipes, spells, and other writings. But as she came to the middle of the book, her eye caught something that made her heart beat faster. It mentioned Bathory's evil ointment! She suddenly found herself turning the pages tracing the whereabouts of the formula throughout the eras. Finally she saw it ended up right here in the very house she was in! After a few more pages, there it was, the whole formula! The recipe for the ointment! So Blanca was finally the witch shrewder than the others.

Eva's heart beat quickened. "Blanca had it all this time, and kept it a secret to protect people like me." Her thoughts were racing. Would one really go mad if one used just a little of it... maybe just a little once in a great while? Could it be improved to become truly benign while retaining its magical powers of youth? If it could, think of the money to be made from such a discovery. Feverously she pulled a pad from her purse and jotted down the ingredience. She was careful to copy the exact amounts to be mixed and brewed.

On the way in the cab, something made Eva tell the driver to take the road through the town of Vashine. When she got there, she found the road wound around the base of a mountain. And there at the top of the mountain she saw it, the Castle of Cachtice and the crumbling tower where Bathory was imprisoned. And it seemed a silent, eerie voice cried out to her from that tower.

Eva suddenly started shivering as though something cold and menacing

enveloped her entire being. As in a trance she told the driver to take her into the village of Cachtice. Cachtice was located at the foot of the long, eerie slope to the castle.

After paying the driver and sending him off, she found herself drawn to the museum in the village. The museum itself was small and presented the history of the village in medieval times. There she saw pictures of the Countess looking young and beautiful in her royal vestments. There were also other pictures and a display of literature about Elisabeth.

Finally she found herself with a group ascending the rugged slope to the ruins of the castle. She arrived to see a mist swirling around and through the ruins; it seemed to take on eerie forms. Her eyes appeared to be playing tricks. The broken spires for an instant appeared to reform into tall towers ascending from the fog; then Eva thought she glimpsed the Countess herself in the swirling mist surrounded by ghostly servants engaged in unspeakable acts. And the wind wailed through the stones sounding like a voice singing to her, enticing her to use the elixir and become beautiful to behold.

When Eva finally descended down the rough terrain, she snapped out of her spell. In a fit of panic she called for another ride and told the driver to take her to the address of her grandparents. She would stay the night, then bid them goodbye and return to the states. There would be no need to tell them anything about the formula she obtained; nor would she question them about her really being a Bathory, sensing how upset they would become.

During the long drive she had time to reorient her mind and think things through. She thought of the ingredience that medieval witches rubbed onto their skin for hallucinogenic effects, herbs like wolf bane and nightshade from belladonna. She would have to be careful. But better even dead than go through life as an ugly duckling with all the feelings of inadequacy that ensued.

Back in the states as a nurse Eva had the chance to stealthily obtain small amounts of blood plasma, which she stored on her refrigerator at home. She also found an occult herb store in the city where she could purchase the witch's herbs prescribed. And each night at home she would carefully mix the herbs with the plasma, judiciously using less of the herbal mixture than the formula called for. She was determined to avoid any deleterious effects from the concoction.

At first it seemed the plasma was not in itself enough. Perhaps the formula needed the purity of real blood. But finally it miraculously started to happen, however at the price of evil dreams, dreams of women being murdered, their blood being drained from their bodies. But she began losing her acne. Then the haggard look was slowly disappearing from her face day by day... The skin all over her body was gradually becoming soft, silky, free of all sags and creases. Standing naked in front of her full-length mirror she admired herself at last. Why, her hair was beautiful and her skin from head to toe was even beginning to glow....

Soon, for the first time she was receiving real compliments and men were beginning to flirt with her. What's more her timidity was leaving also. She was becoming surer of herself and more competent in her work. But her personality was changing in other ways as well. She kept getting what seemed brief flashbacks. They were scenes not of her own life, but of things wicked... horrid things she wanted to expel from her psyche...

One night, she found herself chanting in her room: "O King of cats gather together your felines to lacerate and destroy my enemies. Stay by me. Let me remain healthy and invincible." What I am saying she thought. "I hope to God I'm not going mad!"

And each night scenes of horror kept infiltrating her dreams.... Harlots ravished with whips and chains.... naked women pierced and beaten, begging for mercy.... the ingestion of flesh... the taste of blood... the image of Bathory laughing, blood drooling from her lips... She would wake up in cold sweats, shaking uncontrollably, strangely wracked with guilt...

One morning she awoke with a start, then again felt relieved that the horrors she experienced were again but a dream. But suddenly she sat up in bed, struck with a realization terrible to endure! She was dressed in men's clothes... there was a trace of blood on her hands. Bloody tracks led from the glass patio doors to her bed... She arose from the bed, and in the mirror she saw not her own face, but what looked like the face on the portrait of Countess Bathory.... hair pulled back tightly in a bun. But dried blood covered her mouth and caked on her lips...

Then Eva starkly realized those horrors she experienced each night were not dreams; they could be things she actually did! She started becoming more beautiful because she began using not the plasma but real, fresh blood. She could now remember walking into a house of ill repute dressed as a man, thin cigar in hand, being led into the room of whips and chains where bondage and discipline were performed...

Then were these acts were not enough? In another flashback she saw herself prowling the back streets of the city.... then the prostitute she went with in the alley... and finally murdered! She still had the taste of the flesh and blood in her mouth. In utter revulsion, she stumbled to the bathroom and with her head over the tub could not stop retching long after there was nothing left in her wracking body but the pain of abject loathing and abhorrence......

———————

The police finally traced the murders to Eva Nadasdy (a.k.a. Eva Bathory). She remained incoherent throughout her trial; and was finally sentenced to be interred in the asylum for the criminally insane. Her case was most baffling and intriguing. It took a year of medication and therapy for Eva to finally tell her entire story.

And finally her psychiatrist thought he found the explanation for Eva's almost supernatural transformation from a timid, homely woman to one of beauty and unspeakable atrocity. Speaking with his colleague, the psychiatrist stated: "It was doubtful the witch's herbs themselves did such wonders for her skin; and it certainly wasn't the blood. However, such herbs do have the properties of creating powerful delusions and altered imagery. Could Eva therefore believe she was becoming more beautiful, and even see that image in her mirror? Are you getting that picture?"

The bright colleague picked up on it quickly. "Yes, for one thing: it is quite well known that skin problems caused by stress can be almost miraculously cured by the psyche. For instance, if a susceptible subject under hypnosis really believed an ice cube was a hot stone, an actual blister would appear in his skin. Hence the disappearance of acne and the like could be caused by strong belief in a placebo by itself alone."

The psychiatrist's eyes lit up. "Exactly. The mind itself is a powerful thing. Also, Eva's initial attitude change, her becoming more confident and competent came from believing she was more beautiful. And that attitude in return did make her much more attractive again. She dressed better, stood straighter, looked people in the eye, and her positive attitude shone through."

Then the colleague looked a bit perplexed. "But her final change into a grotesque, vampirish serial murderer... Do you think it was from the final effects of those toxic herbs she rubbed into her skin daily?"

The psychiatrist looked thoughtful. "Yes, those herbs could eventually cause paranoid delusions and hallucinations that could make one violent. It was also Eva's obsession with the Countess Bathory, the historical murderess that took possession of her mind in that state as well. She imitated the Countess' murders quite gruesomely."

The colleague looked bemused. "Yes, that all seems quite logical now. But there are many things about the mind we still don't know.... My own research verified some facts behind Eva's ravings under therapy. There actually *were* many tales... many incidents of vampirism and werewolvery among the peasants in the area of Transylvania for quite some time after the Countess' imprisonment. The heinous acts *were* often blamed on some potion or ointment."

"And what do you derive from that, man?"

"Well, how was it that the peasant witches all serially repeated similar atrocities to those of the Countess herself once her concoction was used by them? It seems to go *beyond coincidence* don't you think? And then there's Eva's direct lineage to the Countess.... Do you think there could be such a thing as the transmutation of souls, the possibility of a departed soul possessing the bodies of living beings? Could the Countess have possibly returned by possessing the bodies of those poor souls and Eva as well?"

The psychiatrist looked astounded. "My God, man! You can't actually believe in such poppycock. Such things can't really happen.... Can they...?"

DESCENT INTO DARKNESS

After his ordination he entered the seminary. There he could lose himself in devout study and prayer. It became a sacred haven of refuge, a place where he could escape in devotion to something greater then the evil brewing within him. At least that was the way it was at first. But when the holy rapture waned at last, the darkness again emerged and with it crept the anguish, the feelings of guilt and self-loathing. Each night his dreams would replay the events leading up to a trauma too horrible to totally recall....

Again torturers were dragging him through the mud... throwing him back into the bamboo hut. Then he would hear the planes again, this time right overhead. To him the whistling shells were the music of liberation. The bombs would either kill him or set him free. Explosions came closer, shaking the ground and everything around him. He could feel the blasts of heat and hear screams of the Viet Cong as the bombs hit home and shrapnel flew.

The compound was in chaos when the hut collapsed around him. Elated, he scrambled away from his confines and into the jungle. From then on he used everything learned in Special Forces to survive. But what did he do in that jungle… in the rice patties…his sense of unspeakable atrocity and horror… the blood spewing into a flowing stream…?

Months later an advancing American platoon found him crouched near a clearing watching them. He was in an altered state, growling and attacking like a wild animal when they approached him. It took many soldiers, some seriously injured, before tying him onto a stretcher.

He was later identified as Staff Sergeant Daniel Dawson, Special Forces Unit 103. But after his body healed, the worst part remained: the panic attacks, the nightmares, the horrid feelings of guilt. PTSD they called it, post traumatic stress disorder. It seemed to come mostly from things happening during his long trek in the jungle. But what it was, he could not recall.

———————

A while after his medical discharge Daniel began visiting Father Brandon, his spiritual counselor in the seminary. Brandon was a wise old man with advanced degrees in physics and psychology. After their initial session the priest realized the profundity of Daniel's disorder. He found Daniel couldn't endure the probing of repressed memories, for therein lurked the danger of full blown psychosis. Psychotropic drugs didn't seem to work either. And Daniel's own attempts at alcohol and street drugs made his condition even worse.

Fr. Brandon switched his strategy to cognitive restructuring. By then Daniel's mind was in dire need of structure; for now he was also going through a crisis of faith with many questions crying for resolution.

"Apart from the horrific acts of humankind, Father, is there such a thing as cosmic evil, a Satanic force that rules the very universe – a power beyond even God."

The old priest at first looked a bit taken back, but then his voice was consoling. "Within the universe at large are the forces of order and chaos, Daniel; but from the chaos comes order. For the power of the Godhead is lawful and the chaos cannot overcome it."

"That sounds intriguing, Father, but can that power from the heavens then overcome the bedlam brewing within me?"

"All of creation is resurrection, my son. And you are a part of it. From the chaos in the beginning came stars and galaxies; from the chaos of exploding stars come solar systems; and from the chaos our own system evolved life in ever increasing complexity. So can't you see it, Daniel? All of nature is resurrection, and you being part of it can also resurrect from the turmoil possessing you now."

Daniel reflected on the old priest's words, which painted a beautiful picture of creation and constant resurrection from turmoil—maybe for even wretches like himself. It seemed even science could agree with such a system in the universe and in nature itself. But the core of the problem again began raising its ugly head.

"I guess the evil I so strongly experience exists not in the heavens Father but here on this very Earth. For here among all living things, is it not true that the strong must always devour the weak....that humanity's history— even religion's history—is soaked in the blood of the innocent? Is it not now proven that only the system of greed and superior weaponry can ultimately succeed in the world of humankind?"

The old priest's air of complacency faded. He seemed to show a brief spasm of palsy and appeared for a moment to experience his own crisis of faith. Then he snapped out of it saying: "Unfortunately on this Earth the gates to the Kingdom are narrow and the road to Hell is wide. As said in the Scripture, Satan is this world's ruler. And I'm afraid such evil power does rule through the greed of the wealthy who make our leaders their whores. It does appear the antichrists continue to rule this world, and a final apocalypse is coming. But human nature becomes evil by it own free will, Daniel."

"Then we are all be damned and doomed indeed, Father. I 'm afraid if all were known we would not wish to stay alive."

"This is where your faith and a positive attitude must become strong, my son. Here is where you must put on the full armor of God so to withstand the wiles of the Devil."

"Will that make the world and God better, Father? Should we then go beyond all the physics and knowledge you've learned and blindly believe in a God-man finally descending from the sky with legions of angels to battle demons and destroy most of humankind. I believe that's the Bible's solution for redeeming all the damage humanity and its leaders have done?"

"That's the literal misinterpretation of the symbols, Daniel. You should instead think in terms of God's Spirit and Kingdom finally rising *within you* to destroy your *own* demons so you can find peace and solace even while on this Earth, ravished as it might be. That's what this counseling and therapy is for."

"It is said that Hell is the absence of God's presence. Is that where Gods' presence is for persons, Father, within the persons themselves?"

"Ah, now you've hit upon the source of your salvation, Daniel – tapping God's Spirit within you, in spite of what's going on out there."

It was beginning to make sense. "Yes, I'm starting to see, Father. But how do I tap into this power I need so badly, even this very moment?"

"You must acquire patience Daniel and learn to do this through meditation, prayer, and good works in the world. Then you will finally realize your own true potentials, your ability to love, and become a part of something more than just a wounded ego vulnerable to this world's pettiness."

"But how long could this take, Father? Would it take weeks, months?"

"Only God knows when that inner power will start to take hold, Daniel. For it to fully take hold might take months maybe years."

"But I cannot wait years, Father, nor even weeks or months. I'm being overcome by an anguish from Hell right this minute, and can't bare it a day longer. Even the proper drugs don't help me anymore. What is left for me to do?"

"Sometimes God is kind, Daniel. It's time for summer break. Practice meditation and inner prayer. Find your true gifts and take them from under the bushel so you can do good works in the world. If things get worse, come see me again Daniel, and we will probe deeper. We will find a way."

———

Daniel maintained a small studio near the seminary. There he could try to recuperate and pull himself together. After a time he found himself thumbing disparately through his marked-up Bible to corroborate something in the back of his mind. His finger fell upon St. Paul's passage stating we are all temples of the Holy Spirit, which dwells within each of us. Then he came upon Luke's passage stating God's Kingdom resides within us all.

Yes. That was it. Fr. Brandon said there were ways one could tap into that greater Power within oneself. It could be done through meditation, or prayer, or good works. Daniel thought maybe he could get lucky and it wouldn't take months or years. Then he recalled a passage from Tyrrell's *Book of Thomas the Doubter*: "Deep within your soul, Thomas, lurks chaos and turmoil. But deeper yet—the Eternal Beauty."

So Daniel forced his thoughts to cease their flow for a time as he became enrapt in meditation. But when his thoughts finally intruded, they were worse than any he yet experienced. Soon they even became audible.... evil voices telling him to do loathsome things.... Daniel sprang to his feet shouting, "No!" He started praying loudly to drown out the foul voices. But soon he found himself cursing God for never intervening to help him ever.

Finally he dropped onto his bed in a cold sweat, breathing heavily and staring blankly at the ceiling. When would it end? How long would he remain at the mercy of his demons within? He finally fell into a fitful sleep of the dammed.

But he awoke before daylight, determined to start anew.

What of good works? He was always gifted in art, a great form of self-expression. Could he create things good enough to sell? Music too! He took many piano lessons as a child and he had an old keyboard stored in the closet. Why not bring it out and play it now, he thought; and so he did.

But the music he created seemed bland, lifeless, forlorn. He couldn't make it express anything more than the mood he was in....

But he wouldn't give up. Later that day he purchased some clay, paints, and an easel at a nearby art store. At home, he proceeded to sculpt and then try painting. But in the end, the art only again expressed his mood: lifeless... forlorn...

Enraged, he destroyed all he created. Was this the way even God felt when He unleashed the flood upon his own creation? With the feelings of a caged animal he paced his room. If the Devil truly rules this world then it explains why he could not get through to God, why he could not create anything worthwhile even after praying to God…

Then damn it all to Hell! If the Devil is present, and God is not – how much easier would it be to get through to Satan himself!

Nightfall crept in through the windows spreading its dark shadows. The moon rose blood red, casting its reflection on Daniel's face, now contorted as one possessed. His eyes shining eerily in the dark, he grasped the phone chortling to himself, unable to stop himself. He dialed 666-H-E-L-L.

On his side, the phone's ringing sounded eerily far away. Then the ringing stopped to the static of an answering machine. From what seemed sounds of uncanny moanings and wailings emerged an echoing baritone voice. The voice gave reminder to all members to appear at the masquerade ball for the Hallowed Eve tonight at 666 Dark Hill Drive in Stormville.

That number again! Strange thoughts crept through Daniel's head. Is this some kind of sick joke? Or is it a sign, a harbinger of change in his miserable life? It was still early evening, and coincidentally Stormville was only about an hour's drive…. Should he go?

Daniel found himself driving down the road toward Stormville. On the way he stopped at a gift shop where he remembered seeing a mask on a stick. That ought to help him blend in a bit, he thought. In a little over an hour, he entered Stormville, and finally found the Dark Hill. Near the winding road's end he saw the gate to a large mansion. On the Gate was the number 666.

Other cars were driving into the entranceway so Daniel drove in behind them. Limousines were letting well dressed people out at the door. He hoped his car didn't look too shabby. The cars parking in the circular driveway all looked expensive. There were Lincoln Town cars, Mercedes, an occasional Rolls Royce.... Once the valet parked his small sports car it was dwarfed and hidden among then others.

No one glanced at him twice when he entered the large hallway. He wrote his correct name, address, and phone-number on the sign-in sheet. What the hell, it wouldn't be bad if someone significant knew who he was or paid him some mind. In the ballroom multitudes of people were gathering in various costumes and masks of all descriptions. A Viennese waltz was playing and many were already dancing.

Holding the mask to his face Daniel strolled to the punch bowl where he could get a better view of the crowd. So all of them are wealthy, he mused. Among them were probably judges, politicians, CEO's celebrities, and God knows who else. When bored they probably had to be imaginative with their celebrative events.

So what in Hell am I doing here, he wondered. Then a tall woman in black was approaching him. With her white skin and long raven hair she looked very much like Vampira in movies of old. "Are you enjoying the party," she said, dipping some punch into her glass.

"I... I find it quite interesting," said Daniel. "But I'm new here and don't know many people," he added, hoping for some kind of break-through. "My name is Daniel."

"And mine is Katrina," she said. "So let me introduce you to someone."

She took Daniel by the hand and led him to a group of people sitting at a corner table. They were dressed in demonic costumes. "This is Daniel." she said to them. He is new here."

A large man dressed like the Devil extended his hand. "Sit down, Daniel and let's get acquainted."

After introducing Daniel all around, the man said, "And my name is Lucifer, but you can just call me

Lewis." There was mirth in his voice, and Daniel hoped this was some kind of joke. Strangely, the man's face seemed to remain always in shadow, never totally visible. Daniel began to feel creepy.

They asked Daniel more about himself, and he told them he was recently discharged for serving with the Special Forces in the Marines.

Lewis then said, "We were playing a kind of game, Daniel, confessing our fondest wishes in life, you might say. Tell me, Daniel, if I could grant you your most fervent wish, what would it be?"

Daniel thought awhile. "Well, I don't know. There's so much to wish for...."

"Come on lad. Why not just say the very next thing that comes into your mind?"

Dizzy from the punch, Daniel found himself almost blurting, "If I could be without fear, without conscience or guilt, I could then be ruthless enough to make it in this dog-eat-dog world."

"Excellent!" said the Devil-man. "Macbeth was right. Conscience *does* make cowards of us all. What do you think of that wish, people?"

A strange chorus of approving murmurs arose from the demonic personae around the table. "Are they traits you lost, or those you never had?" said the Devil-man.

"I was plenty brave and ruthless when first in the Marines"

"And how do you want it back? Do you want it bad enough to offer something quite precious?"

"Like what?"

"Perhaps your very soul?"

The chorus of demons laughed and seemed to moan mockingly.

"What in hell is a soul anyway?" said Daniel. "Whatever it is, it's already damned. So let it stay damned, and the Devil take the hind-most."

Light applause came from around the table. The Devil smiled and looked thoughtful. "What you wish for in this circle could well come true... Yes, indeed it could..." And again came the eerie chorus in agreement.....

The whole scene was becoming too unearthly and unsettling for Daniel. He found himself backing away, excusing himself... heading unsteadily toward the large doors to the hallway. The sights and sounds around him were blurring in a cacophony of confusion and iniquity.

Once outside Daniel breathed in the night air to revive his senses. While driving home he recriminated himself for his loser's attitude. Why did I get so damned spooked, he thought. It was a masquerade ball. People were supposed to seem weird. If I weren't so damned backward and shy I might have made some useful contacts or something.....

WASHINGTON D.C.

Lewis laid the sign-in sheet from the ballroom on his desk and buzzed for his assistant. "Get me a complete rundown on this Daniel Dawson. He could possibly be a candidate for the next classified undertaking." Lewis Bahrenberg exhibited the persona of a semi-retired CEO serving as part time corporate consultant. In reality, he acted as a coordinator of corporate CIA activities, the chief man in charge of top drawer, clandestine action for the government.

When the report came in later that day, Lewis conferred in secret with a small group of colleagues. "This is exactly the type we're looking for, gentlemen: special forces training, sharp-shooter, martial artist, and especially the record of mental illness since his discharge. So far, he stands out on the list."

"We've got to cut the list short and start deciding soon," said a close confidant. "The next assignment is coming shortly."

"Don't worry." said Lewis, "Our agency was always successful in finding the 'lone nut' to be blamed for a major eliminations."

"Yes, it worked quite well so far with King and the Kennedys, among others," said another man, "all within a five year period. So far our propaganda successfully sidestepped all serious investigations of conspiracy. How nicely the way was cleared for the far right to infiltrate the Congress and Senate, even the Presidency, and do so with no major opposition."

Bahrenberg leaned back in his desk-chair savoring their successes. "This is a major coup that is changing the very course of history: All the major liberals: King, Evans, Malcolm X, and the two Kennedys, all extinguished in one short period; and each solved case was pinned on a lone nut set up by the agency with no one ever being the wiser."

"Let's not become over-confident." said another confident. "We must plan out this coming one just as carefully."

Later, Bahrenberg sat at his desk planning his move. "So he needs to regain his courage and ruthlessness.... What I learned when visiting Jamaica might do just the trick...."

Some days later when Daniel arrived home from food shopping his answering machine was blinking. Setting down his bag he pressed the button and heard a female voice with the matter-of-fact tone of a receptionist.

"If you want your wish fulfilled, visit The *Secrets of Shambala* on 311 Wharf Street. There you should find what you're looking for."

Daniel couldn't believe what he just heard. "Damn! Things are getting weirder all the time around here!" he said to himself. "I hope that was real and I'm not cracking up worse than I have been already. But what the Hell, maybe by extending myself and going to that weird party I did change my luck."

Wharf Street was in the sleazy section of town bordering the waterfront. "Great! Now I'm really going from bad to worse for sure," murmured Daniel as he cruised past pawn shops, junk stores, boarded up buildings, a vacant lot, and finally over a corner barroom he saw the sign *The Secrets of Shambala.*

When he left the car he noted the street's population: mainly Blacks, Latinos, and Jamaicans. He climbed one flight up a creaky stairway. When he reached the top a sweet smell blended with the musty hall odor making him a bit nauseous. He knocked on a paint peeled door. It opened by itself.... And there in a room filled with beaded curtains, candles, and incense sat a witchy looking, black woman in an African gown. Her dreadlocks curled and poured out in all directions giving her the look of some spidery Medusa.

"Hello, my name is Daniel Dawson," he said hesitantly.

She appraised him sternly with her one good eye. "Yes, I've been expecting you, mon." she said in a Jamaican accent. "I have something for you." She reached down under her table and brought up an earthen jug; brushing off a cobweb, she sat it on the table.

"This is for you, mon."

"What in Hell is that?"

"It will make you fearless as the lion, clever as the jackal, heartless like the Devil himself."

"Daniel became immediately suspicious. "Where did you get that? Who told you to give it to me?"

"It is a secret Jamaican potion, mon. I was instructed by men in the shadows. They paid me well. Not to worry."

"You say it gives courage? Takes away fears?"

"All fear and remorse will leave you, mon. You will have great power and be pitiless to your enemies."

"How do I know it's not poison?"

The witch poured some of it into a glass then drank it down herself and smiled at him. Multi-colored candle-lights sparkled off the gold in her teeth. If she was Medusa I'd be stone by now, thought Daniel.

Daniel took the jug. "What do I owe you for it?"

"No need to pay, since it's been taken care of. But if you wish to make a donation.... Or I could cast spells for you... or tell your fortune... or make the dead speak..."

"No, I'll try my luck with this first," said Daniel.

On his way out, she took hold of his arm; her evil eye peered into him intently as if reading his soul. "Take care," she said in a foreboding voice. "The power you will receive is capable of great evil, if used carelessly. Take great care, mon..."

Shaking free, Daniel darted through the half open door and moved swiftly down the stairs as if trying to break free from a spell. As he drove away he mused over the potion beside him. "No drugs or drink had set me free yet. Maybe I'll just take a little bit to see what it does... if it does anything at all."

That night after supper Daniel sat listening to classical music to calm his mood. But apprehension crept through him as he stared at the jug on the table in front of him. What if it could take away my depression and fears, he thought. "Hell, anything's better than this!" He filled a glass with the foaming, blue-green liquid. Then, to the strains of a Beethoven sonata, he drank the liquid down.

Its flavor was strong, bitter-sweet, and bubbly. Nothing seemed to happen... until his face and neck started growing warm, as though the bubbles were going to his brain. The warmth soon began spreading throughout the rest of his body. He felt his muscles flexing, feeling stronger...

Then his brain virtually exploded with expectations of things he could not yet define... A feeling of wellbeing... an attitude of devil-may-care flooded through his entire being—as Beethoven's sonata resounded throughout the room, throughout his body, throughout his vibrant, pulsing brain....

He threw his stereo into its recording mode and ran to his keyboard and began to play. Without reading music or remembering tunes he continued playing in a frenzy of inspiration, a furor of creativity bordering on madness.... And so it went on thorough half the night, neighbors pounding on floors and walls failed to break the spell... Then he dropped to the floor in an exhausted, dreamless sleep.

He awoke the next morning in a daze of confusion and wonder as he slowly recalled his maddening experience. "What in Hell was I doing?' he muttered to himself. "I recorded that music I played but it would have to sound awful." He was afraid to replay his recorder, feeling disappointed that the potion would put him into such a deluded and wasteful frenzy as that. "Well I might just as well hear the worst of it," he said as he flipped the recorder on.

"Wait! It's the Beethoven record. No, Beethoven doesn't play like that. It's... it's too dark... too foreboding... But it's as good as Beethoven! It's my own! And, as far as I know... all original! By God, it's great! Such power... Such violence...My music... no longer lifeless and pitiful." Then he looked at the keyboard. The keys! Half of them were shattered and broken! "Oh, God, what kind of demon was it that possessed me last night?"

Daniel spent the rest of the day in a state of numbness and shock, afraid to think of the frightening potentials the liquid possessed. But by evening he found himself again anxious to find out. This time he brought out his easel, paints, and clay. How creative could the liquid make him with these, he thought to himself. Then he anxiously poured himself a glass of the foaming brew, and with shaking hands began drinking it down…

Again the tingling, the feeling of warmth and uninhibited well being. At first he began playing idly with the wet clay, then slowly worked himself up to a frenzy of activity until no clay was left. After that, the paints flew onto the canvass in a furor slashes, thrusts and strokes – one canvass after another until he fell exhausted onto a sofa in the darkness of early morn……

Before noon the next day, Daniel awoke with a start, anticipating what he might find

And there within the chaotic disarray lurked strange sculptures and richly colored canvasses strewn about. On closer inspection Daniel beheld sculpted figures of ghouls and demons in army uniform… pictures of graveyards with body bags and dead victims of war howling in moonlight… monsters and hideous creatures rising from graves for the last Judgment. He further found on the notes he scribbled, his handwriting was slanted the opposite way!

"God! What do I turn into when I drink that stuff— some kind of Mr. Hyde?" He produced this artwork with an originality and creative force he never before possessed. But it looked too ghastly to either show or sell! What was worse, the images stirred things in his unconscious… forbidden things he wanted to keep repressed. A sudden nausea overcame him. He stumbled into the bathroom to vomit out the wretchedness of things best left unknown…

When Daniel recovered, he decided he was using the potion the wrong way. The potion was granting what he craved: It rid him of his fears and inhibitions; and his creative juices were again flowing. But he had better use his new found freedom in ways less introspective and more outgoing. Next time he would take less of it and keep himself more under control.

God, he now had worlds to conquer!

That night after taking some of the potion Daniel ventured to leave his room. Stepping out into the night he experienced a freedom he hadn't felt in years. It was not a freedom from physical confines but from the mental constraints that held him prisoner so long…. Even his senses seemed keener. It just recently rained and he could smell the wet streets, and feel the neon lights beckoning him onward as he strolled through the heart of the city. He followed the sound of soft music into a cocktail lounge, and ordered a whisky at the bar.

While serving the drink, the bartender looked at him strangely. Daniel shrugged it off and surveyed the dimly lit room. He spied an attractive woman sitting alone at the end of the bar. God, even his natural needs were coming back at last. He found himself strolling toward her without constraint.

"Hello, my name is Daniel. Can I buy you a drink?"

She glanced up at him, and her eyes became wide. "No… no thank you," she said abruptly turning her back on him. He noticed she finished her drink with a shaking hand.

What in Hell's going on, he thought to himself. Why are they looking at me like that and acting so strangely? He walked into the restroom and looked into the mirror. And there staring back at him was someone he didn't seem to know… didn't want to know… for the damned face leering back at him had veined, frenzied eyes and mouth contorted into a smirking sneer.

"Who in Hell is that? Who… who am I? Could this be the face of evil?" He heard a husky laugh erupting from his throat. Something seemed to be taking him over, consuming him with lust and an undertow of rage fermenting beneath the surface… He left the lounge and walked the streets as if pulled by some strange energy, a weird force bringing a feeling of dread and foreboding… He seemed to be following primal instincts. Flashes of the jungle came to his mind. For an instant he felt within himself something sub human, a predatory animal.

He finally found himself in a squalid section of town. Skid row bums stumbled in and out of alleyways. Black teens sung rap on the street corner. Prostitutes pranced and sauntered about. Through a barroom window, he spotted a buxom female sitting at the bar. He strolled inside and sat beside her.

"Would you think it too frightening if I bought you a drink?"

She looked at him and shuddered; then a lewd grin broke across her haggard face. "I've seen worse down here, but not much worse than you."

"Well?"

"Yeah, I'll drink as long as you're buying, why in Hell not?

Daniel ordered her a shot and one for himself. At least down here I don't have to be a choir boy, he thought, surprised again at his own wicked laughter. He turned to the woman. "Did you ever dream of forbidden pleasures that exist just for the taking, exotic acts exquisite in their ecstasy and pain?"

She looked at him oddly, and was about to speak when a sharply dressed Latino man stepped between them. "Why ain't you out on the street by now bitch? You sitting here sucking up booze is costing me money."

"I was just about to go, Jose," she said getting off her stool.

"Yeah, and take this with you," said the pimp raising his hand to strike her,

Daniel downed another shot before things went blurry....

——— ——— ———

When Daniel woke up the next day he found himself in a sleazy room. The room was in disarray. His clothes had blood on them. He vaguely remembered twisting the pimp's arm till it snapped.... He was talking to the pimp... telling him..."It's not polite to interrupt..." He was stomping his face... clutching his throat...taking his gun... ushering the whore into a cab... This cheap hotel room... The whore screaming and pleading... What was he doing to her? "Oh God!"

He couldn't remember any more of what happened that night. That was it! Once he returned home he grabbed the jug and smashed it into the sink and stood watching its contents empty into the drain. Better not to think about it. Better to forget it all and go back to his former Hell where at least no one else would have to pay an awful price. He threw his clothes into the wash and staggered into the shower.

But he bought the newspaper that day and found himself scouring through it until he found a small write-up with the heading, "Man Killed in Bar". It told of a man beating another man to death, tearing out his throat, then abducting a woman. The woman was found later that night staggering bleeding and incoherent from a nearby hotel.

The mornings after that, Daniel had flashes of worse things

He would wake up remembering snatches of horrible dreams. And one morning, after dreaming of committing unspeakable acts, he found blood on his clothing again! He was committing those atrocities! But the potion was gone! And he was sure he was staying at home. Was he? My God! The blood! "What in Hell is happening to me?"

He was suddenly overwhelmed with fear bordering on hysteria. He had to see Fr. Brandon again... He had to see for himself just what was inside his soul and taking on such a horrible life of its own. He wondered if it was already too late. He called the old priest, telling him he had to see him as soon as possible...

Daniel didn't tell Fr. Brandon the whole story, just that it was time to uncover just what loathsome abomination lurked within his soul. For if it remained hidden any longer he would surely go completely mad.

Fr. Brandon began pacing and thinking aloud as he made a grim decision. "Extreme situations require extreme measures sometimes. No drug combinations seem to work in the right way, and I don't believe in shock treatments. So... I'm afraid we now have no choice but to go straight into Hell to find your hidden demons and confront them face to face."

Something from within Daniel suddenly felt his face twist into a sarcastic smirk. His voice sounded not like his own. "And where should we find Hell, Father? Shall we start digging into the earth?" God, the monster was trying to surface even now!

The old priest saw no humor. "We will start digging alright, but not into the earth. Hell needs no particular place, for it is a state of mind and being. When the solace of God's Spirit leaves the soul, it then becomes the 'place', a Hell where demons dwell."

"And by demons, Father, just what are we talking about? I mean for real?"

"When the mind and soul become a place of Hell, then the true names of the demons become manifest as 'hatred', 'anguish', 'greed', 'lust', 'deceit', and on …'. When these states remain hidden, the one afflicted can become the tool of evil and thrown into the soul-suffering pangs of a real Hell."

"Phrased in that way, you've described my anguish more vividly than anyone yet. But surely, you don't endorse a literal exorcism in this modern age, Father."

"There are euphemisms. Different therapies call it by special names such as: 'catharsis',' purging', 'abreaction'… even eliciting the 'primal scream' once the core demons are confronted. But regardless of its name— there dwells the danger of not bringing the patient back out of his Hell and thereby eliciting a full blown psychosis. Are you sure you want to go through with this my son?"

"Yes, what other choice do I have but to get this over with, Father?"

"Then arrive here in my study tomorrow at the same time. And may God have mercy on our souls…."

At the next day's session, Fr. Brandon revealed his methods were more scientific than the exorcists of old or of some superstitious practitioners today. "This is legitimate therapy, Daniel. So don't expect the circus performed by tent-preaching evangelists and their gullible subjects," said Fr. Brandon. "I don't expect you to growl or act like a fool."

Instead he tested Daniel's susceptibility to hypnosis and found him capable of fairly deep trance, a capability about two persons in ten possess; therefore there'd be no immediate need for trance-inducing drugs like sodium penethol at this time. "I'm going to find out from you just what occurred in the jungle after your escape, Daniel.

You will remember nothing of what you tell me until we later let it out little by little to bring on your recovery."

The priest then talked Daniel into a deep relaxation, and finally induced him into a trancelike state wherein mental censors weakened their hold. Then slowly the priest regressed Dan back to the time of his escape from the enemy. Each time Daniel resisted, Brandon would relax him again and start over even more slowly... more gradually.

"You are running through the jungle now... You finally become thirsty, hungry. What do you do to survive?"

"I... I follow the downhill slope, for that could bring me to water... I'm right. I'm finally finding a stream... I'm drinking from an old well I come upon, then I'm following the stream. Water can lead to settlements. Animals come to the water as well.... I fashion a crude spear from bamboo.... But each time an animal comes, I'm too weak and slow to kill it.... I trudge on for days... The vegetation could be poison... I know I'm starving...."

"But you are in this jungle for months. How do you finally get food?"

"I... I'm coming upon a settlement.... But I know it's Viet Cong territory. The people will turn on me... turn me in to the Cong ... Stealing food from them will be risky. Even at night I'd have to get right into the settlement. Someone could wake up... sound an alarm... "

"So what do you do, Daniel?"

"I'm hiding... waiting by a well at the stream... Sometimes people come in twos and threes to fill jugs with water. It's getting dusk. A woman comes by herself with two jugs on a stick over her shoulders... Then, I... I'm... No! That's all... That's all... I won't! I can't go on!"

Fearing a psychotic episode, Fr. Brandon slowly brought Daniel out of it. "Okay, you are fading away from the scene now... All muscles relaxing... forgetting the

161

scene... You will remember nothing of what you've experienced... Totally relaxed... Slowly coming out of it... At the count of ten you will come out of it relaxed, remembering nothing...

When Daniel finally came around to normal conscious, he was bathed in cold sweat and breathing hard. But he remembered nothing. His sanity was still intact.

It took many sessions, finally with the help of sodium penethol, before Dan could reveal what happened there by the stream as dusk descended.

"Alright Daniel, you are hiding by the stream now. The woman comes down with her water jugs. What are you going to do..."

"Oh God! I'm shaking from hunger... I feel myself salivating.... I hear an animal growling.... No, no, it's me! There's a growl rumbling from my throat... I'm creeping toward the woman... I'm crouching.... I'm springing onto her back...biting the back of her neck... She starts to scream... I... I'm tearing out her throat... I'm gorging on her blood.... Oh, God...! Oh God...!"

"Then what did you do, Daniel," said the old priest trying to swallow his own revulsion.

"I'm feeding on the carcass... God help me, I'm feeding on human flesh..! Now I'm taking part of it with me to feed on later... Later I will find other settlements. It's a way I survive! God help me, I'm surviving on human flesh as well as animals! And there are worse things... worse things... Now the villagers are searching the jungle... hunting a man-eating fiend... a demon from Hell!"

Fearing a psychotic breakdown, and swallowing the nausea surging in his own throat, Fr. Brandon decided to end the session at that point. "Alright Daniel, your own soldiers are finding you now..... You are now relaxing... forgetting all you experienced... You will slowly come out of it relaxed and forgetting.... relaxed and forgetting...."

For a moment Fr Brandon thought he saw an actual demon in the face of Daniel with lips curled back over bared teeth, eyes with the wild stare of a predator. Then the expression turned to one of panic and terror. "I'm getting flashes now of what happened in that jungle, Father. Horrid glimpses... unspeakable things... horrible acts on animals and people... I can't go on with this, Father. I feel if I do I will go completely mad....totally.... I might never return to being human again."

Fr. Brandon was recovering from his own bout of queasiness.. "Well, maybe we have enough to work with already. There'll be no need to regress you further for a while. We'll just work with what we have at this time."

After Daniel left, Fr. Brandon said to himself, "My God! And there were even worse things? I dare not ask! Perhaps there are things better left forever unsaid, damned forbidden things only God should know." He wondered if he made Daniel's condition even worse. There was a thin line between severe neurosis and full blown psychosis. He hoped Daniel wasn't now on the verge....

Daniel didn't know what to do. Should he turn himself in? But what good would that do? Everything suddenly seemed so damned relative. He received medals for killing better men than a pimp. But all those other innocent victims in the past! And how many more were victims of his madness? Damn it, would he now do it again and again. He had no control over it. How could he stop himself?

The next day, Daniel answered a knock at his door. There were two men dressed in suits. One was heavyset, the other thin and wiry. The thin man showed his badge.

"Mr. Dawson, please be good enough to come with us."

Daniel felt panic. "Am I under arrest? What is this all about?"

"You can call it an arrest. So make it easy on yourself Mr. Dawson and come along willingly." The larger man pulled back his suit-coat enough to show a gun handle petruding from its holster.

As they cruised through the city, Daniel wondered if they were city detectives, or were they CIA or FBI? The car stopped at a large office building. That canceled out city police, he surmised. After riding an elevator to the top floor, he was led into an office.

Behind the desk was a figure looking vaguely familiar. His face remained largely in the shadows. "Welcome, Daniel. I see you were given your wish. Now it's time for payment," he said with a chuckle.

That voice! Now Daniel remembered. It was the same voice he heard when the Devil-man spoke at that elaborate ball.... "Who in Hell are you? Who are these men? What do you represent?"

"I'm the one who took away your fears and inhibitions. It was the wish you wanted granted so badly you would give even your soul for its fulfillment. Isn't that right, Daniel?"

Daniel felt anger well up within him. "All I received was a curse... a curse that has already taken my soul! Are you the one who sent me to the witch! What kind of evil game are you playing here? What in Hell are you?"

"Be seated and relax, Daniel. I have something to show you."

The big man shoved Daniel down onto a chair while the Satanic Lewis brought some enlarged photographs from a desk drawer and shoved them across the desk in front of Daniel. "These are just copies. Other copies are in a safe place. Take a look at these, and tell me what you think."

There in front of him, Daniel saw images of his worst fears come true. The first picture captured him in the act of strangling the pimp he killed that night. The others showed him with prostitutes, doing vile and loathsome things to them."

"Some of those women turned up dead the next day, Daniel. They're on the police blotters. Wouldn't you say we got some pretty clear shots of their faces, and yours with them too?"

Daniel felt both panic and rage well up inside him. "How did you get these pictures? How do I know your own men didn't murder the women afterward?"

"If those pictures get to the right people you will be easily prosecuted regardless. The corpses with bloody bite marks look exceptionally interesting."

Something savage welled up within Daniel; and he sprang for the dark man's throat. But he was stopped by a blow to the base of the scull from behind and thrown back into his chair.

Lewis straightened his tie and composed himself. "From the time we got your case history we knew you were a killer at heart Daniel. Yes, and I knew just what would set you off. Since the time you first took the potion, we had you under surveillance each night. There were men in plain clothes with button-hole cameras and such. We even paid whores to take you to hotel rooms we already set up with hidden cameras."

"But why? What's in it for you?"

"We need persons unknown and unconnected to our agency to carry out rather unsavory activities on occasion. You were chosen for a particular action because you were a marksman in your former profession, and your repressed killer instincts rendered you vulnerable to our endeavors. After all, we had to arrange an offer you actually couldn't refuse."

"Are you saying you want me to kill or assassinate someone?"

"Precisely"

"But why me, when you could probably hire the best? Wait, I think I get it. I'll bet you're looking for something like another Oswald, a disturbed loner to pin it on, so you can continue to remain in the clear?"

"No, no that's not it. If you perform this single deed for us, we are prepared to not only dispose of all copies of these photos forever, but send you on a $500,000 vacation where you can forget about us and our little deal for the rest of your life."

Daniel knew the bribe was a lie, that he would become the perfect patsy. His mind was racing to find a way out. "Why don't you give me some time to think this over?" Where in Hell could I ever hide now Daniel thought?

The dark man waved magnanimously. "Sure, Daniel, there's no hurry. Why don't we have a drink on it to show good faith and wish the best for ourselves," he said as he arose and walked to a bar in the corner of the room. "What will you have?"

"Whisky." Daniel sensed danger, but he had to humor them, hoping they'd let him leave this one time. It would be all he needed. They clinked glasses in a salute and he took a drink.

But soon the room was swimming before him. His legs no longer held him. He started to collapse... and all went blank....

———

He regained consciousness on a bed in a seedy room. His same two abductors sat watching him across the room.

"Where in Hell am I now?" His head was throbbing.

166

"Bolivia, in La Paz." said the thin one. "We were flown here by private plane. You'll carry out your mission tomorrow. Today we will run you through it and show you what you'll do."

"Bolivia! You bastards! You slipped me knockout drops and brought me all the way here?" He came at them, only to face two drawn guns and was told to sit down.

"I didn't agree to do the dammed thing yet," said Daniel, now shaking with rage.

"You were told there will be a hit. The name is Archbishop Helder Camara. He's been giving talks that are stirring up another damned revolution, and right after we finally disposed of the Commie, Che Guevara and dispersed his guerillas. The beat goes on."

"Why in hell do we have to bother with all this crap down here?"

We have big natural gas and oil contracts here. If the Commies take over it all goes down the drain--not to mention potential chain-reactions throughout other countries down here. Hey, you're doing a patriotic duty for your country. Think about it that way."

"Yeah, I'm thinking all right." He was thinking how ironic it was that he was trying to become a priest, and now he's being forced to kill an Archbishop! He sold his soul alright. Devil in Hell here I come. Christ, I'm long overdue.

His two captors must have been warned or his martial arts ability; for they always avoided coming into his arm's reach and flanked him on opposite sides, their hands near their holsters. In the car he was to strap himself in the back seat on the driver's side while at gunpoint from the front passenger's side out of his reach. They were experts at what they did. They drove through La Paz to a large building by the town's square. They led him up a back stairway to the roof, which overlooked the square.

"See that podium they're setting up over there," said his captor. That's where the bishop will be giving his speech tomorrow at 7 PM. You'll be given a high powered rifle with a telescopic sight. You're a marksman. You can't miss. You're escape is arranged for you. After that you'll be given the money and your ticket to freedom."

Daniel was silent, but his thoughts were racing from the time they left the roof and on the ride back. They probably had one or two of their own shooters ready for this job. His real part would be to play the patsy – the one to be caught or even killed while the real killers got away. Why else would they go to all the trouble to force a nobody, a sicko like himself to do the job?

He had to plan his escape. They would probably take shifts to watch him tonight when he slept. That would be his best time to make his move. But he was still being overcome with those spells at night without warning, without the dammed potion. Tonight he had to keep himself under some kind of control.

Before midnight the thin one said he'd stretch out awhile in the adjoining room while the husky one would keep a four hour watch on their prize. The big guy sat across the room by a window, gun held in his lap, occasionally watching the street scenes below.

Daniel then felt the inhuman fury welling up inside him. He rose up from the bed, his face distorted in a sinister smirk. "Well, when you got to go, you got to go."

The man looked at him strangely. "You're going to the bathroom, right? And why are you speaking in a hiss? What in Hell's wrong with your face? It looks contorted?"

"Yes, it's time to go." Daniel was now leering at the man, feeling the uncanny rage continue to rise behind his twisted grin.

"Make it quick. Leave the door open." said the big man, fondling his gun uneasily. "Don't try anything. They don't appreciate scraping people off the walls down here." The big guy started laughing at his own joke.

In one leap Daniel was on the man tearing out his throat."

Hearing the commotion the thin man awoke and entered the room gun in hand. Daniel now had the gun and was behind the propped-up larger man as a shield.

They exchanged gunfire.

Most of the thin man's bullets struck his own colleague while Daniel's bullets struck the thin man in the chest and between the eyes. The man dropped to his knees, then pitched forward to the floor. Daniel noticed blood coming from his own wound where a bullet grazed his neck.

Pure instinct remained as Daniel retrieved the car keys from the dead man and raced down the back stairs to the car. As he drove away he knew people heard those shots. The proprietor is probably in that room already.

He drove like a demon toward the outskirts of town and on through the night. He finally took a dirt road into a wooded area before he passed out from exhaustion and loss of blood. When he awoke in the morning, he found he could again think calmly and carefully.

Once the police were notified it might not take long before they knew the make and license plate of the car he's driving; for the corrupt government authorities, at least the higher ups, must be in on the whole murderous scheme. And he already knew too much to be allowed to roam free, not here, not back in the states, not anywhere anymore.

Hell, if he didn't ditch the car soon, they'd catch him anyway. He had to find refuge and get away. But how, where? Maybe an airport. But he had no money, and they'd soon be watching there too. There's always a bus but each bus would be searched. And though he wasn't too far from the Peruvian border to the west, he didn't have a passport or identification and they would be watching at the borders as well. He could emerge at an unwatched area of the border from the jungle…..

Then an epiphany came to him. Why in Hell would he want to survive anyway? He was a God damned night stalker and killer! He committed atrocities! And he would commit more if not stopped. Yeah, some of the men he killed were worth killing. But what of those innocents? The system had long since transformed him into a damned killing machine!

Then the full realization came upon him: He had already sold

his soul when he joined the service to take part in the mass slaughter and destruction in a bogus war. For the corporate industries behind the wars and the entire US government, especially its shadow side, truly comprise the Satan who rules this world. The deranged and demented like himself are but the human waste, the fecal byproducts of that great evil machine…

His best recourse then would be to make his peace with God as best he could, then leave the civilized world. How "civilized" was it anyway? He was ashamed of the species of which he was a member. He was ashamed of himself for letting its Satanic rulers consume his soul He drove away and stopped at the nearest township to phone the La Paz police and warn them about the assassination scheduled for 7 PM that day. Luckily the one on the other end spoke a bit of broken English. Hell, even if the police were in on it they now had to realize the plot was known, and therefore might call it to a halt.

Now that he made his peace it was time to return to the primeval realm where he first gave up his humanity. Yes, once you are soulless that's easy to do, he mused to himself as he headed east toward the Bolivian mountains and rain forest. It seemed a savage and mournful voice was calling him there, a voice only he could hear.

Hours later when the back roads would take the car no farther, he embarked into the jungle on foot. When out of bullets he would have to hunt in more primitive ways. But he was already a predator, a subhuman slaughterer. Since he had long since resigned from humanity he must now follow his natural course of devolution—or was it Devil-lution? He chuckled at the stupid joke.

In the distance he heard the raucous growl of a jaguar, his competitor, and felt a low rumble in his own throat returning the call. As he trudged farther through the mountainous jungle leaving the remnants of civilization far behind, the last verses of Faustus came to his dwindling human consciousness.....

"The stars still move. Time runs. But the clock has struck. The Devil has already risen and Faustus is damned. You stars who reigned at my birth—now draw up Faustus like a foggy mist into the enthralls of your clouds that when you vomit forth into the air my soul may ascend to heaven..... Ugly Hell, gape not..... Come not yet, Lucifer!"

INTIMATIONS OF THE HOLY

A ROSE IN SPANISH HARLEM

Julio was feeling uneasy as he walked through the black hood to Deno's place. He didn't like some of the looks he was getting. If only his skin wasn't so damned light. Why couldn't it be dark like his brothers'? Nervously, he sifted through his pockets and brought out a joint, then paused in a deserted doorway to take a few tokes.

Things began to get mellow once more. By the time he took the last drag he was feeling pretty cool. As he strolled on his way, the eyes following him from the crannies of the hood looked somehow less evil now. Maybe all the uptightness lurked only in himself, he thought, not really in the people on the street. Yeah, that's where it's really at. You create your own evil, man.

As he rounded the corner a splash of scarlet struck his eyes. He looked down and there he saw a rose glowing like a crimson jewel on the steaming asphalt. He picked it up and reverently and tucked the stem into his belt then sauntered dreamily on his way. "Yeah," he mused to himself aloud. "The world is really a mellow place. It's just the way you look at things. It can be any way you make it seem."

Even the four black chicks wearing gang jackets didn't seem unmellow as they headed toward him—not even when an inner voice reminded him the girl gang bangers could be even more evil than the guys. He strolled on whistling soundlessly, thinking about the rose. The heftiest chick moved well out of her way to bump hard into him.

After he regained his balance Julio only smiled and made to move on, but the other girls blocked his way. Something in him whispered they were often heeled with blades and together could cut him to pieces in no time. Hell, if a little kid got bold with you in this neighborhood you wouldn't have a prayer.

"Don't you watch where you're going, motherfucking white boy?" the hefty one screamed at him. "Where do you come off bumping people on this street?"

But Julio remained strangely cool. No fear or anger welled within him. He simply leaned back easily against a building and regarded his predators calmly

"Don't you answer when you're spoke to, pale ass bitch?" The big one was working her and her friends up into a mean frenzy. "Well you can stay stupid after I cut your thing off for you, baby."

The rest of them laughed as she swaggered toward him to the tune of, "Yeah!" "Get him, Bert!" "Fix him where it is, babe!" Something was flashing in her hand.

Maintaining his strange cool, Julio reached inside his belt. The big girl stepped aside defensively, cocking her blade. The others moved in on him menacingly.

Then, with all the gallant chivalry of a cavalier, Julio bowed down really low and offered Big Bertha the rose.

Her eyes got big. The other girls stopped, gaping in their tracks. Bertha's hand snatched the rose. She looked at the flower, then at the pale boy. Her eyes grew even bigger. "Lord have mercy!"

The hostility in her face began to crumble. The other chicks began tittering like school girls. Then the big girl's bosom began bouncing and rocking with the rhythm of her laughter till tears streamed down her ebony cheeks. The hostile watchers on the street began laughing too.

Julio grinned at them all. Then waving gallantly he strolled along his way. "Yeah," he said for anyone to hear. "The world and people are like you make them, man. That's where it's all really at."

THE SEEKER

A Hindu youth walked sadly up the dusty path leading from his village; for he had hidden away to listen to the elders privately speak of mysteries the tribe must never know, especially the mystery of Maya, of all earthly things being but illusions in the minds of men.

So there are ultimately no such things as beauty, goodness, and truth as we know them. Were not the prized arts and treasures of one culture but oddities and trinkets to another? Was not what is good and the true among one people distasteful or false among others? For true reality lurks hidden beneath the veils of Maya. He remembered them all nodding in solemn agreement while stroking their billowing white beards in omniscient contemplation.

The mountain path wound to a low cliff overlooking the valley. There he paused to look out upon whispering fields of tall grass waving amber in the setting sunlight. The scent of wild flowers in the breeze filled his very soul with intoxicating fragrance. But a tear crept down his cheek. For he remembered the words of the wise men:

"And is not all we behold even in nature merely the illusion of Maya? Does it not all exist only in the mind and senses?" they would ask. "For animals with senses more keen than our own, must surely perceive things differently – each species perceiving a different world –

as does our own. Who then beholds the true world out there?" they would ask with the wizened heads solemnly nodding.

Dejected, the young lad walked on. The emerald green of the dew-laden forest with its songs of many birds made him only sadder. If all these exquisite sounds, scents, and colors exist only in my mind, he thought, how then can I ever know *true* beauty? After a time, the upward winding path led the youth to a frosty line where the forest ended.

The air became thinner making his head light, his senses deceptive. As the night shadows fell he began to question the use of his aimless wandering. He was about to turn back but saw a flickering glow further up the trail. A strange compulsion overcame his caution; he approached closer toward the light.

Then he stopped to behold an old man in a tattered yellow robe squatting by a cave. A fire played its light eerily about the man's gnarled features. Cautiously the youth approached closer to the ancient figure. He seemed older than even the elders of the village, for his hair and beard were longer and whiter and billowed more wildly. Could he be even wiser as well?

Gathering all his courage the youth walked over to where the man was sitting. But the old one did not look up. He remained sitting cross-legged, gazing it seemed into fiery dimensions not apparent in the space around him. His face appeared enrapt in serenity beyond contemplation.

"Pray tell, ancient one," cried the youth impulsively. "Forgive my brazen interruption of your meditation..." He dared not say more, and was for a long time met by silence. Finally, without looking up or changing his gaze, the old one spoke:

"What so troubles your mind, young lad?"

The youth was startled a bit, for the shaking voice seemed unearthly and far away as if emerging from another world, another time. Then the youth regained his composure. "You who appear even older than my village elders and seem a holy man, I have come to beg your advice."

"So then speak, young one," came the strange, ancient voice sending a chill of excitement through the youth.

"I am seeking out in quest of beauty, but not its mere illusion as dispersed through the senses of creatures and minds of men. I seek what is truly beyond such limitations."

The distant voice again thrilled the youth. "It is rare that one so young seeks the truth beyond Maya."

The youth for a moment stood proud. "My teachers already claimed me a prodigy who will one day become a wise elder." Then he looked sad again. "But I cannot wait for that now. For unlike my young peers I already understand I live in illusion. Now I am no longer content with my present experience, yet I lack the higher wisdom to transcend it."

Sitting immobile the old man answered. "Though your understanding is keen for one so young, you still hold but only a fragment of truth, my son." So distant was the voice the youth had to bend his head close to the old man's lips to hear it.

The old one peered deeply into the fire as if seeing the past and future manifest in the dancing flames. His words came slowly.... "Once your world of Maya was pierced by the first ray of truth, the pleasures of kama deserted you. Yet you now seek just beauty, which in Maya you equate only with the senses as if true reality is one glorious sensuous experience."

The flames sparked and danced, reflecting wild strobing patterns onto the face of the aged oracle.

Strangely his lips appeared motionless as the ancient voice continued. "But the quality of experience you seek depends on your present stage in Maya. If you through ignorance have deluded desires, then the ability to transcend mundane experience is weakened."

The youth felt at once perplexed and saddened, His voice was apprehensive. "You mean my present stage of experience is not enlightened enough to attain liberation?"

"Not enough to attain total liberation," came the venerable voice. Then the old one's expression changed. "Neither was my own experience sufficient when I was but a youth in days of old." His eyes looked thoughtful as they peered deeply into the flames, as though reflecting back thorough eons of time….

"Yes, it was when I was struggling with Maya in the deep, dark forest when the avatar, Brahma Sahampati, helped me achieve enlightenment and full liberation in this lifetime…." Then slowly he directed his gaze onto the youth. A strange feeling crept up the young man's spine, as though a field of force was penetrating his entire being. He could swear he saw no lips move as the old one spoke.

"Come sit down before me, young lad."

For an instance a chill of reluctance seized the youth, an urge to flee back to the safety of his mother's hut. But the voice again insisted. "Sit here before me son. Do not be frightened." The gentle voice reverberated through the youth's body like a great mantra, and he found himself kneeling powerless before the venerable sage as the voice filled his mind.

"Stare deeply into these old eyes, my son, and tell me what you see."

The youth found himself compelled to peer deep into those ancient eyes… and soon he felt his entire being drawn out from his body into swirling, limitless depths….

"Tell me what you see, my son."

"I... I see endless realms of mystery strange and unknown..." His voice seemed to come no longer from himself. "I feel lost within eons of time swirling from eternity... from the Void...Shunyata!"

Then a primordial voice seemed to surge from an infinite sea of consciousness... from the very edge of eternity itself.... "The veils of Maya will soon be lifted from your inner eye, my son. Even now the delusions of ignorance are leaving you. Thusly your present stage of development is rapidly moving forward. You will soon be ready to transcend ordinary experience, and achieve liberation in this lifetime...."

The youth felt as if cobwebs were being swept one by one from his mind's eye as if every cell in his brain was exploding into awareness. He was both frightened and ecstatic.

"You will continue to ascend the mountain. Near the top you will find a wide ledge overlooking the valley. There you will build a small fire. Meditate profoundly on the flame. Become oblivious to all else. Your mind and the fire will become one. When the flame finally snuffs out – so will all your illusions of self – and you will know your Source, you will emerge reborn onto the liberated path. Arise now my son."

A strange illumination came upon the youth. Unsteadily he arose, his awareness suddenly coming frighteningly acute. The old man held his gaze as he spoke. "Remember carefully my son: Once your mind becomes purified, you must then reflect and meditate upon your experience to find your karmic path in this life, lest the light of illumination leaves you."

"Is there anything more, O venerable sage?"

"I will reveal to you a foreshadowing of what your new enlightenment will present to you: There can be no beauty with goodness, nor can there be goodness without truth. Go now and find your way."

The old one then released the youth from his gaze and once more became immersed in the unearthly serenity of his own contemplation. The youth paused a bit longer to look upon the old one sitting before his fire enrapt in wisdom and fulfillment surely denied most living beings.

And through his new awareness, the youth was astonished to behold what appeared a soft, glowing light shining around the old soul before him. As the aura grew stronger, it seemed to emanate a peace passing all understanding.... Then and there the youth knew that in his lifetime he had witnessed a true saint... an avatar!

He turned from the holy vision to traverse the path winding upward toward the summit of the mountain. The thinning air made him lighter headed and did strange things to his mind. Ethereal images appeared, dancing eerily in the moonlight urging him onward.

When at last he approached near the summit, he finally found the ledge. After preparing a small fire, he sat in lotus position. At first he found it hard to still his mind with all its thoughts and questions. But after a long while his mind was soon lost within the flame, oblivious to time and surroundings. He finally became conscious of naught but pure awareness... uniting as one with the fire .... becoming purified of all thought and image. Soon he could no longer distinguish his consciousness from the flame – it became a flame – flaring bright and strong,.

Eventually the flame and consciousness began to ebb. Finally, only a sparking ember remained. When the ember snuffed out, so did his last spark of self.

Then something exploded soundlessly in the back of his consciousness as it moved beyond self... beyond Maya... beyond all limitations of awareness.... There was no longer mind or perception. Without sight, he became all light... without hearing, all vibration pulsing and exploding into otherworldly dimensions... He finally knew the ground of pure being... the clear light of the Dharmakaya... beyond all bliss...

Over the valley's horizon the sun rose lazily as a red fiery ball. Its scarlet light played about the sleeping face of the youth sitting in lotus position before the smoldering embers.

He startled awake, his eyes slowly focusing upon the valley below him. And he beheld a brilliance and richness surpassing all color and form. He never thought such beauty possible as it scintillated and vibrated all around him; and with it came an experience of a Truth transcending all words and images. And from within him came the revelation that here was truly the hidden essence of nature and the cosmos shining through it all. The village elders called it Brahman.

Then he remembered what the old sage said to him: "There is no beauty without goodness, or goodness without truth." And he did finally behold ultimate beauty and truth by shedding the veils of Maya. But what of goodness? How can the beauty of truth lead one also to the good? I will find the answer when I again meet the old one on my way down the mountainside he thought. So he followed the long, winding path downward until he came to the campsite of the ancient one, but found no one there. Only the gray ashes of the fire remained.

The youth then seated himself where the old one once sat in meditation and prayed aloud to the spirit of the missing sage: "O venerable sir, you have removed my veils of Maya and shown me true Beauty as the essence of reality – the Truth - shining through all things. But now it's time to find my karmic path. How can I do so without a true knowledge of Goodness leading the way?"

Then came a voice, whether from within him or beyond him, he could not know: "With the veils of Maya lifted, you have reached the first stage of Nirvana, my son. You can now behold Beauty shining through all things. And these are the keys to goodness, the end of all suffering. For those who reach this stage of Nirvana have the ability to heal and enlighten others, and hence have true beauty of goodness shining through them as well."

And so another revelation from the old one had come into the youth. The emanation of beauty into reality is from the limitless potential for the good. And likewise the true beauty in persons dwells not in their perishable surface qualities but from the goodness, the benevolence within them shining through.

Then it struck him: Although he himself had become illuminated, what of the millions of beings suffering in the unenlightened ignorance of Maya, their minds and senses dulled…their lives deluded, unfulfilled as they exist as but brief sparks over the eternal flame.. Could there be absolute beauty while there is still unspeakable suffering in the world?

And again an inner voice came to him in that holy place: "Now you have received the light, my son. My long life was spent in showing many others the way. Now I must live on in you. Is not your mission clear now, my lad?"

But then a feeling of unworthiness befell the youth. "Am I, who am still so young, truly capable of this responsibility? Will this enlightened consciousness within me not fade away with time?"

"It's time again to arise, lad. And fear not, for to ignore your mission is to lose the light. Arise and go to the mouth of the cave. There you will find my robe." The youth walked to the cave and saw the robe laying there seeming strangely luminescent in the darkness.

"Now put on the robe, lad."

Reverently he adorned himself with the robe, and immediately a new source of strength and courage surged through him.

"Now go in peace, my son," came the soundless voice now within him. From now on you walk in my footsteps. Your life's journey will be long and demanding. But I will walk on in you."

He walked out into the light. The illusory world of Samsara was never more beautiful as he strolled serenely down the mountain path. "Very pretty this Maya," chuckled the young sage amusedly. But soon he was enrapt in contemplation of a deeper beauty as he walked down the winding mountain path. After he descended the mountain he came upon a mournful procession of cowled monks walking slowly passed by him. Strangely their robes were like his own. He approached the monk nearest him.

"Pray tell O venerable sir, what is this sad occasion?"

The monk turned, and his grieved eyes looked quizzically at the young man beside him. "You who wear the yellow robe must surely know this is the funeral of the Master.".

"The Master?" said the youth, a strange unspoken knowledge rising within him.

The monk's tone was both perplexed and admonishing.

"Where have you been, man? The dying Master, Gautama, requested he spend his last hours meditating alone in the wilderness above the mountain forest so he could transcend Samsara, the cycles of life and death, in the highest stage of Nirvana. Just before sunrise we carried his body down the mountain." The monk turned away and waked mournfully onward.

The youth stood for a moment stunned by this overwhelming realization. The old sage on the mountain was Gautama, the Buddha!

Light in the head and weak in his knees, the youth reverently pulled the yellow hood of the Buddha over his head and humbly joined the procession. The glow of this realization now burned so strongly within him he could hardly contain his mind. But soon he was calmed again by a profound sense of purpose and peace.

And the holy voice reverberated soundlessly through his entire being: "From now on you will walk in my footsteps. Your journey will be long but I will walk on in you…"

THE SECOND COMING

In the dark of night two men hunched together speaking in hushed tones on the deck of a seaside cafe. No one could hear them over the waves crashing on the Italian shore. Just for a moment Cardinal Mercedes could not contain himself.

"At last, the return of the living Christ!"

Then he looked around nervously and continued in a hushed voice. "I managed to gain entrance to the hidden vaults in the Vatican's lower chambers. And I now have in my possession the original Sudarium, the bloodied cloth thrown over the face of the crucified Christ. This is the hidden one said to be far more authentic than to the cloth residing in the Oviedo Chapel."

"Ancient bloodstains contain the most difficult DNA to reproduce," said the scientist, DeGarmo. "However, with my improved method of revitalization, the chances of success are good."

"I've taken the whole cloth, not just a piece of it," said the cardinal. "That way, if one specimen doesn't work out to your standards, the cloth can offer plenty more."

"Will they soon miss the cloth and send out an alarm?" said the scientist becoming a bit nervous himself.

"The treasures in the vaults are seldom inventoried. Many are not looked upon for years. But by then, we hopefully will reveal a prize that would shock and change the entire world!"

"Yes, we might soon be holding the history of the world in our very hands."

"Are you sure you can perform this amazing task without deformities to the embryo or harm to my sister?" said the cardinal.

The scientist smiled reassuringly. "I, over and above all the rest, can guarantee a high probability of success. They now can easily clone sheep. However I, Joseppi DeGarmo, have finally achieved one hundred percent success with primates using my newly developed formula and technique."

The Cardinal shakily downed another wine. "But this DNA is ancient, man. You say you actually have a new way of revitalizing the DNA in a petri dish before injecting it into the prepared ovum?"

"Yes, and that's how we will bypass the many cloning failures and deformities occurring in past attempts with old DNA."

"Excellent!" The cardinal's eyes were wide with excitement.

The cardinal then leaned forward, his gaze intense. "You must realize secrecy is of utmost importance. Even the boy must not know until he is out of seminary. We certainly cannot have scientists, reporters, and the public swarming all over us."

"Of course, I will not take any of the credit until the secret is exposed. I have other experiments, some of them human, in the meantime."

The cardinal leaned back fixing the scientist in a piercing stare. "Of course you will not, senior. For if such things were to be claimed prematurely, the cloth would be destroyed and all would be denied. No scientist would want to look so foolish in front of his peers I'm sure."

"As long as you pay me well for this, the secret will be kept until you are ready, Monsignor.

"Good," said the cardinal handing the scientist a packet under the table. Here is 45,000 lira for now, and the rest will be yours once the baby is delivered healthy and alive."

"Thank you, Monsignor. I will need all the funds I can acquire if my own groundbreaking work is to continue...."

It was less than a year later. In the delivery room of a New York hospital a small cult of believers were electric with excitement. There was Cardinal Mercedes just in from Rome, His brother, Father Lorenzo, a parish priest, and his brother-in-law, Professor Antonio Barete whose wife was in labor delivering the child. The scientist, DeGarmo had implanted the DNA in her ovum in a private laboratory outside Rome. The birth had to occur far from the omnipresent eyes and ears of Vatican City.

Then the miracle happened. The child came out alive from her womb. But there was bad news. The boy was born a blue baby and had to be incubated. They all realized clones were notorious for being stillborn or born deformed or prone to sickness or death. This one formed from such ancient DNA made recovery seem all the more impossible. The live birth itself was a miracle.

For what seemed an eternity the small group remained in anguish. Would it all come to naught with the new born merely perishing? Was it even meant to be? They all continued to pray incessantly for days that turned to weeks. Then finally, the news it seemed from heaven was bestowed upon them all. The baby was at last in adequate recovery and ready to be nursed at home. They realized surviving against such impossible odds made this recovery a great miracle indeed!

The scientist, DeGarmo was paid well in return. The sacred cloth was returned to its vault, three fourths of it fully intact. They named the child Thomas, which in Aramaic ("Taoma") means "twin"; the apocryphal texts claimed the disciple Thomas as Jesus' spiritual twin.

It was soon noticed the child was precocious. He skipped grades in grammar school, and graduated from Catholic high school early. Instead of engaging in sports, he seemed to pursue an unquenchable thirst for knowledge.

And, with his stepmother a librarian and stepfather a professor of anthropology, he learned a lot at home as well as in school. After becoming president of his senior class, he showed real talent in speaking as well.

He was found to have something of a genius IQ. And throughout his school years his step uncle, Father Lorenzo, visited often and was strongly orienting Thomas toward a priestly vocation. Cardinal Mercedes would visit from Rome also whenever he could free himself from his duties in the Vatican.

Only one peculiarity stood out: In an Italian family, Thomas looked awfully Jewish. They all reasoned that yes, Jesus himself was Jewish but he was the founder of Christianity wasn't he? So the orientation is appropriate, is it not?

By the time Thomas was entering college he was already psychologically primed for seminary and the priesthood. And he followed his orientation well: graduating from liberal arts college summa cum laude, and from a Jesuit seminary with the highest honors.

Now with the foundation completed it was time to inform Thomas of his holy heritage and true calling. It was in a private chapel where his step- parents and two step uncles gently informed him of how he became the identical twin of Jesus. The cardinal bent close to the shocked young man. "Do you realize that once your DNA is revealed to match the blood on the cloth you will have a clear way to become the next Pope and could influence the entire world to change its runaway self destruction? Why the possibilities are endless!"

Thomas stood frozen with confusion and wonder. "I can't really believe this. How could you ever prove to me this is true?"

"All we have to do is match your DNA with that of the cloth's blood to prove it. The chance of error is one in millions."

"But, there is no way in this world you can tell me I am God! Why, this is a sacrilege! Am I not a walking desecration of God?"

The cardinal laid his hand on the young man's shoulder. "Of course you're not God, nor are you a desecration. You simply have the genes of Jesus as a man. If this be sacrilegious let me the instigator of it all take full responsibility before God."

Thomas paced back and forth before the alter, shaking his head in disbelief and awe as his step family sat breathlessly waiting for his reply. Finally he turned and spoke to them.

"This... This is too sudden and too big a revelation for me to respond to at this time or any time soon... I must have more time to contemplate such a great responsibility."

"Of course," said Cardinal Mercedes. "After all, once he found his calling, Jesus himself had to spend 40 days and nights in the wilderness to think it through. What would you like to do?"

Thomas seemed in a trance as he wrestled with the shock of his revelation. Finally he spoke. "What you have laid on me now is so big... so grave.... I would like to spend some time in a monastery to pray on this and contemplate this great burden brought upon me."

"I and Father Lorenzo could arrange that easily enough," said the cardinal. Where would you like to go, and how long would you need to stay?"

"I would need some isolation... privacy... a hermitage in a Trappist monastery. For how long, I do not yet know."

———————

In the monastery, He took on the name of Brother Taoma, his name in Aramaic. He put in his request to dwell in a hermitage. When the request was granted he took his residence in a hut in an isolated, wooded area where he could study and meditate on his mission in seclusion. He was brought only food and drink, and occasional requested book. Otherwise he was left completely alone.

There he would contemplate and reflect on all he learned from Christian and religious history, and biblical criticism, and theology, and philosophy, and the sciences.... He became particularly interested in Eastern and Western mysticism and studies of Judaism as well. He finally asked for books on Kaballah.

As the months went by he was finally spending most of his time in silent meditation. Then one night the epiphany struck him. It was a virtual explosion in his brain when all knowledge seemed to come together in one symphonic unity, a virtual harmony of multifaceted meaning. He felt a warm, vibrating glow as a stream of light beamed down through the trees and played upon him until he could actually see an aura shining forth from his body.

Now was the time to break silence, and re-enter the world.

His step family greeted him warmly, they were electrified with excitement. Cardinal Mercedes brought Thomas to Vatican City and there called a meeting with a group of scientists. After grinding red tape and a final permission from the Pope, the cardinal at last had them test and compare Thomas' DNA with the DNA on the sacred face-cloth taken from the vault.

The match was perfect. The Pope was notified. News spread wildly first throughout Vatican City and Rome, then throughout Italy, then Europe, then the entire world.... Teams of scientists retested the findings, and none could refute it. The DNA match with the ancient blood became an irrefutable fact.

It was not known whether to punish Cardinal Mercedes or put him in line for the papacy. And the scientist, DeGarmo could now proudly take full credit for such an amazing scientific feat as this; he was spoken of as a genius and soon was in line for a Nobel Prize.

Thomas now had to take refuge in a secret, guarded area of the Vatican, for seas of reporters and masses of people clamored to meet him. There in that sacred haven he was often visited worshipfully by the Pope himself, and they discussed many things....

Of course arrangements had to be made for this holy prodigy with the very blood and likeness of Jesus to speak to the world. But the Pope was nervous. In his conversations with Thomas he felt he was getting all the wrong answers... answers that went against the Catholic faith.

In his meeting with the cardinals the Pope said: "This Thomas had the audacity to say the solution to our priest shortage and clerical pedophilia is to allow both marriage and women into the priesthood. How could he! But after all, this is not the original Christ himself. Could it be that the blood became somehow contaminated after two

195

millennia of dormancy? Before Thomas is allowed to address the masses, perhaps it would be wise to have him interrogated by a panel of experts to see if his mind was also contaminated, as it were."

When Thomas heard he was to undergo a clandestine inquisition he balked and secretly left the Vatican under cover of night.

For a long time no one knew the whereabouts of Thomas. With Thomas' absence the Pope's mood swung from confusion and anger to chronic depression. How fantastic to have the clone of Jesus himself in the Vatican and then have him just disappear! But Jesus' manifest likeness seemed to have ideas of the anti-Christ! And he looked so Jewish! Meanwhile Cardinal Mercedes and Thomas' step parents were wracked with worry bordering on panic. Where in the world could he be?

———

He walked the streets of the poorest countries. Soon the presence of a strange prophet and healer was known by those in filthy shacks unfit for life, poor wretches lying in gutters and back alleys, those in the dimly lit hovels of forgotten souls. He ministered to homeless children who ran in packs by night, to prostitutes who wandered dreary neon streets. He learned the different languages as he traveled the world, and would preach to the poor of love, and the injustice of those with wealth and power allowing such pitiless poverty, such unrelenting pain.

Soon there were many tales of a humble healer helping the poor, working in soup kitchens, healing sick souls by laying his hands upon them. Wherever he went, bands of the desolate began followed him about: the homeless, the mentally ill, the prostitutes, the addicts.... A touch of his hand, the look in his eyes seemed to impart miraculous healings upon these forgotten wretches of the world.

Thomas finally emerged on the Mount of Olives at the Garden of Gethsemane in Jerusalem. There at the Church of all Nations (the Basilica of Agony) he arranged to speak on worldwide video. Cardinal Mercedes with great relief finally caught up with him and helped with the arrangements. The world was finally notified.

The world's leaders and many high in the ranks of both religion and academia vied for a chance to confer with this living phenomenon born from the ancient blood of Jesus. On the day of the sermon, Thomas presented his talk standing on the very bedrock where Jesus was said to pray. A multitude of people crowded the site. All the TV cameras focused upon him.

"My brothers and sisters: Let me start with the distinguished academicians of today in our highest halls of knowledge. My careful studies revealed your *modern* thought has finally corrupted down to nothing. It began with high humanistic ideals. Then it devolved to existential self-centeredness and pragmatic expediency, then to postmodern relativism, and finally a mindless nihilism and heartless materialism with no humane values at all: the philosophy of the sociopath!

"And I have walked the streets of the poor and oppressed, the multitudes exploited by those whose values rest only in greed and power. So I say to you world leaders: We've seen the devolution of a Communism that too often oppressed the poor it would have helped. And we see it now in the ruthless exploitation in Capitalism whose leaders pretend religious piousness while worshiping only the corporate greed that bought their souls. Now Mammon becomes the true God and Satan the real ruler of this world. And he rules it through its rulers. For Satan is in truth the darkest side of the rich and powerful who have always oppressed the masses.

197

"And from the wars for profit, from the rich exploiting those who have not, with half the world starved and enslaved—this darkness now blankets most all of humankind. "Now I say to you dictators, and also you leaders of Capitalism, and all you political whores in high places for the corporate greed mongers—through your worship of Mammon you continue to crucify the poor of the world.

"And what has Christianity done about all this? Its history is soaked in the blood of the innocent, of poor wretches hanged and burned alive for being different, of crusades and religious wars that mass murdered tens of thousands. Even to this day the fundamentalists condone the horrendous evils of war to the tune of 'God and country" although it was said in Malachi 24: 7 and Isaiah 2: 4: *"Nations shall not lift sword against nation; neither shall they war anymore."*

And you who refrain from loving deeds—who think you will be saved by 'faith alone'—your lack of benevolence condemns you and the world around you. For the best friends of evil are those good people who do nothing about it.

"And in the U.S. you the pious do everything to destroy birth control among the indigent and starving masses. Your influence helped create overpopulated conditions worldwide where the poor have to sell even their children into prostitution and slavery. Even in the U.S. the poor continue mass producing children on welfare without fathers: the girls becoming pregnant at age 13, the boys making killing fields of our inner cities and overpopulating our jails and prisons.

"I too am against abortion. But must I declare to you what is obvious? *The greatest deterrent for abortion is birth control.* And if these words are not heeded— greatest abortionist will be God himself! For overpopulation among the poor will always bring on the wrath of famines, plagues, and wars. We have seen films of such afflicted populations with starving babies, flies crawling on their little faces. Where is such atrocity taught to you in your Bible? Adam and Eve were told to be fruitful and multiply *because there were no other humans on the Earth at that time!*

"But by the time of the New Testament we find Jesus saying on his way to Calvary *'Daughters of Jerusalem, do not weep for me but weep for yourselves and your children. For the days are coming in which they will say: Blessed are the barren wombs that never bore and the breast which never nursed!'* (Lk. 23: 28-30) And in the Epistles we find: *'Rejoice O one who does not bear. Break forth and shout, ye who are not in labor; for the desolate have more children than she who has a husband.'"* (Gal.4:7)

"And what is all this outcry about family values? Even the most bigoted war-monger and murderer can have love for his own family, clan, or tribe alone. Moreover, clannishness begets bigotry, hatred for those who are different—and can even expand into jingoistic wars. Therefore Jesus said; *'If you love those who love you, what reward have you? Do not even the tax collectors do the same? And if you greet your brothers only, do you do anything special?*

"As we remember in Luke: when asked 'Who is the neighbor we should love?' Jesus then gave the parable of the Good Samaritan, *who was actually from the enemy tribe.* Such teachings are especially sacred in this shrinking world; for if all diverse tribes, cultures and religions do not soon reach out beyond themselves with the tolerance necessary for peace—your self-created Armageddon of world destruction will soon be upon all of you indeed.

"I say this also to the fundamentalists *beyond* the Christian world. I say it to the Zionists who displace masses of Muslims from their homes in the Holy Land. I say this to Muslims who suicidally mass murder innocent civilians in the name of God. All who blaspheme by committing such evil in God's name— worship not God but Satan!"

In the filled cathedral there was a great hush. And millions, perhaps billions sat fixed on their TV's in hushed silence and awe...

"Now I say to all you fundamentalists: Desist from your bigotry against women and those who are not like yourselves. Desist also from your doctrines that overpopulate the world with the starving poor. Desist from displacing and mass murdering those of other faiths. Your absurd, literal interpretations of Scripture create a plague upon the world. For the verses you chose to emulate are not from God but inspired by the Devil—who loves to be worshiped as God.

"And to you the wealthy and the world leaders I say: desist from your worship of Mammon. Your greed in the guise of sanctimony destroys the world. Desist from your wars for profit that mass murder innocent civilians in lands not your own. Desist from your ruthless oppression of the poor both abroad and at home. For even now you are stirring an undertow of hatred among the masses that will someday explode in a worldwide apocalypse of your own making."

Dictators and Capitalist leaders in the audience sat red faced. Some were whispering in the other's ear. The leaders of the religious right started yelling "Anti Christ! Anti Christ! Crucify him!" An evangelical leader stood up and said to the others. "Now that the Antichrist is here at last, the apocalypse at Armageddon will soon arrive, and this Antichrist will be crushed in Jesus name!"

Taoma, the image Jesus, looked in shame upon the scourge of humanity. "Perhaps I should say some words on the true Armageddon. You who think you will be raptured: After the nuclear blast you will indeed disappear; you will end up as sunspots on crumbled walls! Or perhaps in disgust God will do it all himself: The good Book says a dragon will sweep with its tail stars down to earth; there are meteors and comets with tails out there predicted to one day fall toward you all.

"Maybe there will there be a millennium of peace when, from the radiation and the sins of your fathers, thalidomide-like mutants pitiful to behold will be thrown back into another dark age of merciful ignorance? Then will a new race of homo pollutants be born? The term "sapien" (the wise) could never be proudly be used again.

"Perhaps there could even be a time when the elite could flee in space ships leaving behind this ravaged Earth they have finally destroyed. They could ride out beyond the cratered slagheaps and poisonous gas-balls of our solar planets... out past the sun's lake of fire... .never to see the ruined paradise of our blue green Earth again.... As it is written: '*The sons of the Kingdom shall be cast into the outer darkness... There they will weep and gnash their teeth.'* So shall the Devil—found in man—be finally cast out into that eternal Abyss forevermore.

"This will be the fate of your grandchildren and great grandchildren if you who teach, preach, and rule do not change your ways. There is no cheap grace—no redemption without repentance. Jesus did *not* die *for* your sins—he died *from* your sins. He resurrected in the hearts and minds of those who would follow him—those who would die to their sins with him and resurrect with him to a better life. And so it should be with the followers of holy martyrs from all great religions. So woe onto you who teach nihilism, or preach bigotry and superstition, or rule to enhance only yourselves from the war-mongers and greed-mongers of the world."

Afterward, there did seem an undertow of reform starting even in the universities. Scholars (Professor Berate in the lead) were no longer so glib in disclaiming absolutes in the ontology of truth nor were they so quick to claim all values relative in worth. And in the highest circles there were also intimations that there may in fact be something like purpose or meaning for the universe after all.

Also, the fundamentalists seemed no longer so anxious for Armageddon to commence; and the Roman Church began paying more heed to its parishioners and the strife in the world. However, after telling the world the truths so long suppressed by religious and secular leaders, those in charge were not happy. Thomas received death threats from Christian and Muslim fundamentalists alike. He was condemned by the Jewish Orthodoxy. He was finally excommunicated by the Pope.

Moreover, it was leaked that the CIA now had a contract on Thomas for exposing corporate greed and the imperialism of the American way. In clandestine meetings secret agents searched for solutions. Perhaps they could find a religious kook (one who would murder abortion doctors) as a patsy to carry out the assassination; or would professionals be more efficient?

More than one philosopher stated that if Jesus ever did return, this wicked world would crucify him once more.

———————

Meanwhile, in a hidden Jewish temple Taoma's final intent was to not become the Pope but to reestablish his Judaic roots and return to God.

A squat team broke into the last place Thomas lived. But they found him and his belongings gone.

Taoma finally delved deeply again into the practice of Kaballah. In his meditation his soul entered the gateway of *Shekinah* in ascending the ethereal tree of life.

Sinister men began questioning all who had seen him last. But no one could tell where he had gone.

As he shed his animal spirit (nepesh), he experienced his soul (neshama) being carried upward by his heavenly spirit (ruach) until he reached the stage of the *Tiferet* where his soul obliviated and merged with the resurrection of new being in the cosmos.

Agents could find no trace of Thomas in Europe or in the States. More agents were searching his whereabouts in the Near and Far East.....

At last he came he came into mystical union with *Binah*, the Cosmic Womb of Creation at the threshold of *Ein Sof*, the Source Mystery of all Eternity, what mystics might call the Godhead.

And finally they burst into the inner sanctum of Thomas's refuge. They fired their weapons. He fell back against a wall, arms outstretched at his sides. As the living image of Jesus slid down to his death, on the wall remained the bloody imprint of the cross......

Special Note: References to the papacy above alluded to situations before (and most probably after) the current reign of Pope Francis, who at last tries to emulate the true teachings of Jesus.

CPSIA information can be obtained at www.ICGtesting.com
Printed in the USA
BVOW11s1818200514

354009BV00007B/131/P

9 781621 374862